CIVIL SERVIC

CIVIL SERVICE REFORM

Building a Government That Works

Donald F. Kettl
Patricia W. Ingraham
Ronald P. Sanders
Constance Horner

BROOKINGS INSTITUTION PRESS
Washington, D.C.

Copyright 1996
THE BROOKINGS INSTITUTION
1775 Massachusetts Ave., N.W., Washington, D.C. 20036

Library of Congress Cataloging-in-Publication data

Civil service reform : building a government that works / Donald
F. Kettl, . . . [et al.].
    p. cm.
    Includes bibliographical references and index.
    ISBN 0-8157-4903-1 (pbk.)
    1. Civil service reform—United States.   2. Civil
service—United States.   I. Kettl, Donald F.
    JK681.C5 1996
    353.006—dc20   96-25251
                                                       CIP

                    9 8 7 6 5 4 3 2 1

The paper used in this publication meets the minimum
requirements of the American National Standard for
Information Sciences—Permanence of Paper for Printed Library
Materials, ANSI Z39.48-1984

Typeset in Times Roman

Composition by Linda Humphrey
Arlington, Virginia

Printed by Kirby Lithographic Co.,
Arlington, Virginia

⒝ THE BROOKINGS INSTITUTION

The Brookings Institution is an independent organization devoted to nonpartisan research, education, and publication in economics, government, foreign policy, and the social sciences generally. Its principal purposes are to aid in the development of sound public policies and to promote public understanding of issues of national importance.

The Institution was founded on December 8, 1927, to merge the activities of the Institute for Government Research, founded in 1916, the Institute of Economics, founded in 1922, and the Robert Brookings Graduate School of Economics and Government, founded in 1924.

The Board of Trustees is responsible for the general administration of the Institution, while the immediate direction of the policies, program, and staff is vested in the President, assisted by an advisory committee of the officers and staff. The by-laws of the Institution state: "It is the function of the Trustees to make possible the conduct of scientific research, and publication, under the most favorable conditions, and to safeguard the independence of the research staff in the pursuit of their studies and in the publication of the results of such studies. It is not a part of their function to determine, control, or influence the conduct of particular investigations or the conclusions reached."

The President bears final responsibility for the decision to publish a manuscript as a Brookings book. In reaching his judgment on the competence, accuracy, and objectivity of each study, the President is advised by the director of the appropriate research program and weighs the views of a panel of expert outside readers who report to him in confidence on the quality of the work. Publication of a work signifies that it is deemed a competent treatment worthy of public consideration but does not imply endorsement of conclusions or recommendations.

The Institution maintains its position of neutrality on issues of public policy in order to safeguard the intellectual freedom of the staff. Hence interpretations or conclusions in Brookings publications should be understood to be solely those of the authors and should not be attributed to the Institution, to its trustees, officers, or other staff members, or to the organizations that support its research.

Foreword

REINVENTION, downsizing, and restructuring have become mantras on both ends of Pennsylvania Avenue in the discussion about remodeling the federal bureaucracy. However, who will manage the system and what skills and structure they need to run it effectively have received little attention so far.

This publication of the Brookings Center for Public Management addresses these issues and outlines how the federal civil service can respond to the changing demands upon the government and carry us into the next century. The authors grapple with maintaining the nation's historic preference for a merit-based personnel system, while introducing the flexibility, partnership, and incentives for excellence needed to build a government that works.

This book brings together leading academics and practitioners of civil service policy to chart a course for the future. Donald F. Kettl is director of the La Follette Institute of Public Affairs at the University of Wisconsin-Madison and a nonresident senior fellow at Brookings. Patricia W. Ingraham is professor of public administration and political science and director of the Campbell Institute of Public Affairs at Syracuse University. Ronald P. Sanders is director of the Maxwell Center for Advanced Public Management in Washington, D.C. Constance Horner is a guest scholar at Brookings and former director of the U.S. Office of Personnel Management.

The authors would like to thank Thomas E. Mann, Alan Campbell, James P. Pfiffner, Bert Rockman, and Joel Aberbach for their timely and constructive comments on a draft of the manuscript. The authors also thank Theresa Walker for editing the manuscript, Carey Macdonald for providing invaluable research support, and Julia Petrarkis for compiling the index. Financial support for this project was provided by a grant from the Ford Foundation.

The views expressed in this book are those of the authors and should not be ascribed to their institutions, those people whose assistance is acknowledged above, or to the trustees, officers, or other staff members of the Brookings Institution.

Michael H. Armacost
President

June 1996
Washington, D.C

Contents

CHAPTER ONE

The Case for Reform

THE IDEA of a merit system, applied uniformly to all federal workers, has been the foundation of the public service for more than a century. The patronage of the late nineteenth century has cast a long shadow across American politics. Since then, the drive to protect government—and those who manage it—from the spoils system has driven four generations of policymakers.

However, the federal government's uniform merit system today is neither uniform, merit-based, nor a system. It now covers barely more than half—56 percent—of the federal government's workers. Only 15 percent of the federal government's new career employees enter through the system's standard testing-and-placement process. Worst of all, the civil service process too often hinders, not helps, the federal government as it struggles to get its work done. Problems of recruiting and retaining good workers, many government managers believe, have worsened service delivery and hurt productivity.[1]

A vast gulf has grown between the laudable purpose for which the civil service was created—building a good, professional executive free from political interference—and what it has the capacity to accomplish. To make things worse, a thin veneer of time-honored principles, venerated with almost religious fervor by government employees and elected officials alike, protects the civil service system from careful scrutiny. Under this veneer, however, the system is badly crumbling from neglect. Quite simply, the federal civil service system is no longer up to the job of managing what the federal government *must* manage.

Yet behind this stark crisis is hope. Even though the 104th Congress (1995–96) proved one of the most partisan on record, one issue survived the interparty, interbranch battles with barely a scratch: government reform. In fact, a remarkably broad (if basic), bipartisan consensus maintains that the federal bureaucracy must be fixed.[2] Government officials and academics alike have agreed on five fundamental principles:

—a system that builds much-needed, often-lacking capacity to solve government's tough new problems;

—a system that rewards creative, high-performing civil servants with better pay;

—a system that provides civil servants with far more flexibility instead of the current system's dysfunctional rigidity;

—a system that holds civil servants accountable for that flexibility with tough measurement of their performance; and

—a system that develops and encourages strong leadership by career officials to protect and promote the public interest.

But if there is such strong consensus on what needs to be done, why has it not been done? Because, quite frankly, most observers of government view government management in general, and civil service in particular, as an issue that is as dull as dishwater. To raise civil service reform is to induce quickly the MEGO (my eyes glaze over) phenomenon. Civil service reform is on everyone's list of jobs that must be done— but it is high on virtually no one's list. It has too little sex appeal to excite political interest; and, though everyone agrees on the need for change, the consequences of *not* reforming the civil service never seem great enough to force it onto the policy agenda. It tends to be an issue, therefore, that policymakers put off until a better time, and that time never arrives. Meanwhile, government civil servants struggle with an increasingly dysfunctional system whose costs steadily grow. Coping incrementally has introduced even more bizarre variance into a system whose greatest strength has long been its uniform adherence to high principle.

Although civil service reform can seem the most boring issue in the world, it is critical because it permeates everything that government does. Government's performance can only be as good as the people who do its work. When it fails to recruit, retain, and reward the best possible people—or when it subjects good people to bad systems—government's performance inevitably suffers and taxpayers lose. The Internal Revenue Service, the Federal Aviation Administration, the Defense Department, and the National Weather Service have each made multibillion dollar mistakes because they did not invest in enough of the smart people needed to manage new computer systems.[3] The California attorney general has investigated the intrusion of organized crime into a casino owned, but not managed closely enough, by the Justice Department's Marshals Service.

In these and too many other cases, the federal agencies simply did not have enough of the right kind of people, in the right places with the right tools, to get the job done. The federal government is trying to use early steam-engine-era administrative technology to govern an information-age nation. It is little wonder that, far too often, programs struggle or fail, citizens are disappointed by results, money is wasted, and public distrust in government grows. It would be unfair to lay all of these problems at the civil service system's doorstep. But it would be folly to try to fix them without first fundamentally reforming the system. Government's problems are mounting, and they are increasingly rooted in people problems. Only a people-based solution can solve them.

The road to better results is now so full of potholes that more patching will only make things worse. What the civil service system therefore needs is a complete reconstruction, from the bottom up. The new system ought to build on the ten steps to building a government that works, which are outlined in figure 1-1 and are developed more fully in the pages that follow.

The job will not be easy. Although the dysfunctions created by the existing civil service system are huge, their costs are not obvious. The same was true in 1986 in the case of a bridge crossing a deep ravine on the New York Thruway. To motorists who used the bridge daily, all seemed well on the

Figure 1-1.   *Ten Steps to Building a Government That Works*

1. *Redesign the federal government's central personnel agency.* The Office of Personnel Management needs to be reinvented to define and promote the fundamental values of government service. The central office needs to inculcate these values, promote high performance, collect critical data on how well the system works, and especially ensure adherence to the system's core objectives. It also needs to define the values to be followed.

2. *Ensure flexibility in choosing how to do government's work.* Existing rules provide some protection against political interference, but at huge cost in inflexibility. Government needs to find a more productive balance between careful protection and good management.

3. *Rely on whoever, inside or outside government, can best produce the federal government's goods and services.* The government needs a strong core, but it does not need to produce all its goods and services itself. That work ought to be done by whoever can do the job best—the federal government, state and local governments, private companies, or nonprofit organizations. The government ought to be agnostic about *who* does its work but care deeply about *how well* it gets done.

4. *Insist on accountability for results.* Whoever does government's work ought to be held responsible for doing it well. The government needs a high-quality, performance-based management system tied directly to its people system.

5. *Manage government's producers by new forms of contract.* If those who produce government's goods and services are to be given greater flexibility, contracts with teeth that bite—strong financial incentives for good performance, financial penalties for poor work—ought to ensure that the government gets its money's worth.

Figure 1-1. *(continued)*

6. *Reward good performance through performance-based compensation.* High-quality work ought to be rewarded through the government's pay system, as well as through nonfinancial incentives like opportunities for advancement. Government's workers must have the incentive to take risks and perform in superior fashion.

7. *Equip government with a powerful core.* The federal government needs a strong and permanent capacity at its center—a small but effective corps of highly skilled managers—to ensure it always acts as a smart buyer of its goods and services.

8. *Build a culture of performance through career development and rotation through different work.* The values of government's permanent career staff need to be reinforced through a significant investment in training. Workers, moreover, need to rotate through a variety of positions, in government and in contractors' offices and in the offices of state and local governments who often do government's work, to give them the perspective they need to be highly effective managers.

9. *Cultivate a culture of public service.* More than anything else, a culture of strong leadership will ensure that taxpayers receive the results they deserve from government. The federal government needs to transform the Senior Executive Service so that it provides continuous, high-level leadership for the bureaucracy.

10. *Integrate the civil service system more tightly into the federal government's other management systems.* The civil service system cannot stand alone. It must be closely tied to government's other management systems, especially its budgeting and performance systems.

surface. But underneath the bridge, years of corrosion had slowly eaten away its structure until it could no longer support the loads it had to bear. The bridge collapsed, taking motorists to their death and crippling the area's transportation system. The civil service system today finds itself in the same position: on the surface, it manages to cope; in its foundations, it is slowly decaying; and in its performance, it is simply unable to continue to bear the burdens it must carry. It must be fixed, and the fix will require more than a shiny coat of new paint.

Despite the unquestioned need for reform and the broad consensus for doing something, building the kind of reform the system needs will not be simple. Reformers will have to resolve daunting dilemmas: pressures for a downsized government that have not been accompanied by downsized expectations for services; devolution of more federal power to the states, which will complicate the job of ensuring accountability for results; expansion of contracting out, with more nongovernmental partners producing governmental services; and citizen expectations for ever more responsive programs and congressional demands for better performance. Reformers will have to lessen the tensions between government's workers and its managers and will have to grow a new generation of leaders to shape the government of the future. Government cannot avoid tackling these problems. Its current management systems are not even close to doing the job. No reforms, including the proposals in this book, can fully solve all of these problems, but strategic reforms in the right direction can dramatically improve government's ability to do what must be done.

The issue that seems so boring to so many, therefore, is critical because the issues are central and inescapable. Nevertheless, career civil servants, public employee unions, and members of Congress have a strong, vested stake in the status quo. Even though no one really likes the system's idiosyncrasies, the inside players have at least learned to cope with them. The dysfunctions are far more comfortable than the uncertainties that real reform would bring. Moreover, many of these insiders have built a powerful interest in protecting their own special power, which flows from their ability to negotiate the system's arcane rules. Change brings risks, and the risks are greatest for those most directly affected. The entire nation would unquestionably benefit from real reform, but no one has a clear stake in championing it.

But the job must be done. It must be done because the civil service system touches everything in government. If it does not work well, neither can anything else in government. Too often reformers have sought to tinker with the civil service system for its own sake. This book argues that the civil service system needs to be viewed instead as a tool to accomplish a far more important end: building a government that works. Government needs a tool carefully honed to get the job done. This book outlines a plan for real civil service reform, for creating a high-performance government, and for underlining everyone's stakes in success so clearly that the risks can be overcome and the barriers flattened.

CHAPTER TWO

The Federal Government's People Problems

PRESSING NEW PROBLEMS have pushed government right off the map charted by existing public systems, organizations, and processes. Many government officials have been surprisingly inventive in devising new ways to solve these problems, but too often the existing management systems have handicapped them in struggling to adapt. A generation ago, government struggled under the systems' constraints. Today, the systems have proved totally inadequate for solving policy and management problems. They will barely provide the foundation for what the nation needs to manage the government of the future.

The federal government's traditional management systems no longer solve today's management problems well. They were built for a hierarchically organized, authority-driven, "one size fits all" government that relied on clear organizational structure, rules, and arm's-length relationships to command and control its programs. However well these systems once operated, they are ill-suited to the task of managing in an uncertain, chaotic, and competitive world. Government has grown ever more complex, but policymakers are struggling to steer it with oars long since obsolete. It is little wonder that government sometimes seems rudderless.

For more than a century, the civil service system provided the linkage between federal policymakers who steered and federal bureaucrats who rowed. Over the years, however, the linkage between policy and results has frayed and cracked. The civil service system was created in large part to eliminate patronage for all but high-level government jobs. It has achieved its original purpose well; the perils of the spoils system, about which Progressives complained in the 1880s, have largely disappeared from the federal service. However, the drive to protect the system from patronage has gradually made the system harder to manage. The tensions between its original mission—*protection*—and its current one—*performance*—have grown so large that they gravely threaten the management of public programs.

These tensions are scarcely new. Indeed, any civil service system that simultaneously seeks to protect employees and to manage programs has an inherent contradiction. The search for protection produces rules and generates inflexibility; the search for performance demands results and requires flexibility. Reformers have tried to solve this problem by tinkering constantly over the last century with the system's rules. The constant, incremental changes, however, have gradually pushed the rules from the means to an end—better government—to ends in themselves. The rules have frustrated the very workers the system was designed to protect; the performance problems that have resulted have left them vulnerable to political attack.[1]

Many federal agencies, frustrated by the constraints of the current system, have won sweeping authority to create their own new rules and systems. This authority, however, has often been granted without central supervision or a means to ensure that agencies pursue the central principles that have guided the system for more than a century. Neither has the Office of Personnel Management (OPM) redefined what its new role ought to be in a more flexible system.[2]

Real reform therefore cannot come from the two most obvious options. Rewriting the rules at the center will not work because the system must solve new management problems that rules themselves cannot solve. Operating agencies need considerable flexibility to match the basic rules with their own missions and management processes. On the other hand, delegating full responsibility to executive agencies to establish their own systems, as the Clinton administration has proposed, can only multiply the confusion. The civil service system is not only a means of management but also a mechanism for transferring and promoting deeply anchored political values. The center must have a role in anchoring agency-based flexibility in these values.

Neither extreme—rule-based centralization or agency-based devolution—is the answer. Moreover, the nation is far past the point at which continued tinkering can solve what has become a deep and serious problem. The costs of government management problems are mounting. These management problems, moreover, are increasingly rooted in people problems, and only a people-based solution can resolve them. The experiences of agencies experimenting with new flexibility, coupled with the experience of nations abroad and private companies at home, suggest the shape of the government's human resources management system of the future: a government that knows where it wants to go but is flexible about how to get there.

Neither strong central control nor unbridled devolution can work. What government most needs is a fresh means of sailing the ship of state: improved steering at the helm, and a better way of guiding the rudder. Sketching such a plan is our aim in this book.

Problems to Solve

Such a plan must solve five deep and serious problems plaguing the civil service system:

1. THE CHANGING NATURE OF THE FEDERAL GOVERN-MENT'S WORK BADLY STRAINS THE CIVIL SERVICE SYSTEM. Most elected officials, journalists, citizens, and even some top government managers behave as if government operated like a gum ball machine: insert a coin into the top and services come out the bottom. Indeed, the assumption of a control-based chain of command, from the top to the bottom of bureaucracy,

through a hierarchy controlled by authority, is the foundation of public management. It has long been viewed as the path of efficiency; when reformers throughout the twentieth century sought to improve government, they typically resorted to restructuring its operations in the belief that better organization would produce better results. It has also been the central mechanism to ensure accountability; for a nation eternally suspicious of political power in general and bureaucratic power in particular, the system provided a means to exert democratic control over government administrators. The gum ball model seemed simple: create programs, insert money, delegate power, and then stand back to let the machine produce results.

As simple and powerful as this logic is, it has one basic problem. It does not even remotely describe how the federal government actually works. Only about 4 percent of the federal budget goes to programs that match the traditional gum ball model: services that the federal government directly delivers. In the other 96 percent, the federal government writes checks for payments to individuals (58 percent) and interest on the national debt (15 percent). It contracts with private companies for goods and services (13 percent). It makes grants to state and local governments (5 percent). It fields the armed forces (5 percent).[3] Most government, in fact, operates through proxies—private and nonprofit contractors, state and local governments, and individual citizens—who produce the government's goods and services.[4]

This is not to say that hierarchy does not matter. It surely does; no matter what else, hierarchy describes how government agencies are organized, how the reporting arrangements work, who is responsible for what, and how appropriations and programs come together. It does not explain well what government does or how it does it, however. Instead of directly producing goods and services, most workers within the federal bureaucracy work in networks: with other federal employees in other federal agencies with whom they are jointly responsible for a program's effectiveness; with grantees in state and local governments who arrange goods and services;

and with private and nonprofit organizations who deliver many goods and services. That presents a very different kind of management challenge.[5]

An Internal Revenue Service (IRS) computer modernization project, devoted to processing returns faster and answering taxpayers' questions better, is instructive. A General Accounting Office study found that the IRS lacked the ability to think strategically about its information management needs, to design the systems it needed, and to manage the modernization process.[6] The problem, Representative Jim Lightfoot said, was not high technology. It was, rather, "a lack of effective management." The IRS certainly needed to buy new hardware and software to deal with the increasing demands of the tax system. To build and design the system, the IRS relied on contractors, but the contractors became a patchwork instead of a single integrated system. IRS officials were unable to oversee the design of the system, adequately monitor the contractors' performance, and ensure that the government got its money's worth.[7] The General Accounting Office concluded that the $8 billion effort "to modernize tax processing is jeopardized by persistent and pervasive management and technical weaknesses." In fact, the GAO reported, the IRS was moving ahead "with little assurance of successfully delivering effective systems within established time frames and cost figures."[8] It would be one thing if the problems had only happened in the IRS computer modernization, but the same thing occurred in the multibillion-dollar Federal Aviation Administration's air traffic control system and the National Weather Service's computer modernization projects. In case after case, the government has not built the institutional capacity to ensure it could adequately manage the proxies through which it spent the public's money and in which to put the public's trust.[9]

The stark reality is that many sophisticated observers of government believe in the model of the gum ball machine, a perspective that simply does not match reality. When problems arise, therefore, reformers often understand neither the problem nor the best solution. Even worse, because they act on the

assumption of hierarchy, reformers often tinker with the structure in ways that make problems worse. By pushing the wrong
buttons, they risk sending the machinery of government lurch-
ing even further out of control.

The problems are certainly not unsolvable; skillful managers throughout government have had surprising success in
tackling these very problems. At the Zablocki Veterans Affairs
Medical Center in Milwaukee, for example, managers teamed
social workers with physicians to improve outpatient care.
Contract managers determined how to buy medical and support equipment and supplies smarter, cheaper, and better. The
Department of Energy's Hanford, Washington, lab saved $29
million over four years by improving security at a former
nuclear weapons production facility. Better management of a
Defense Logistics Agency pharmaceutical inventory reduced
costs by $48.6 million. In each case, the key was moving from
traditional hierarchical control to more effective alliances
within government, and between government and its intergovernmental and private partners.[10] Reform requires hard-wiring
the flexibility to innovate and the lessons of these innovations
into government's routine, not forcing managers to struggle
constantly against standard operating procedures.

2. THE CURRENT CIVIL SERVICE SYSTEM STRUGGLES TO
PRODUCE AND RETAIN THE SKILLED PROFESSIONALS GOVERN-
MENT NEEDS TO PERFORM ITS WORK. These tasks require highly skilled workers matched to the jobs that the federal government must perform. The federal government, however, has
struggled mightily to recruit and retain the workers needed.

Over the last generation, the federal government's changing mission has dramatically changed the makeup of the work
force. Blue-collar employment has dropped sharply, from 26
percent of the federal work force in 1973 to just 16 percent in
1993.[11] The white-collar work force, while roughly constant in
size, has become more diverse. In the years from 1960 to 1980,
the number of engineers on the federal civilian payroll
increased by 50 percent. The number of computer specialists

increased by more than 600 percent and continues to rise.[12] The creation of new agencies, such as the Environmental Protection Agency, and new departments, such as the Department of Energy, stimulated the demand for more scientific and technical expertise in government. The need to recruit and retain physicists, biologists, oceanographers, nurses, statisticians, botanists, and epidemiologists, as well as large numbers of engineers, lawyers, and accountants, now preoccupies federal personnel managers.

It is very difficult to determine just how serious the government's recruitment and retention problems are. The OPM has not kept careful records on the issue since the late 1980s, and other data are fragmentary at best. Indeed, the lack of good and timely government manpower statistics simply underlines how far federal policy on the work force has slipped; even rudimentary planning is impossible without basic information. A collection of snippets, however, continually reemphasizes the basic point.[13] Because the federal classification system has not been systematically reexamined since the late 1940s, it has been that long since the system has had an overhaul. New skills, like computer programming, have been squeezed into the existing system. Low pay has made it hard for the federal government to retain its work force.[14] When the Clinton administration and Congress agreed in 1993 on a buyout to reduce the federal work force, the average grade level of employees accepting the buyout by retiring early was GS-11, the very people on the verge of becoming the government's upper-level managers for the future. Such managers were, of course, the target of the Clinton administration's pledge to halve middle management. The federal government, however, had invested years in training these managers for top positions, only to lose their rich experience—and to move blindly into the future—without devising an alternative strategy for producing the next generation of upper-level managers on whom the performance of government programs would rest.[15]

The most profound data, however, come from the testimony of today's government workers and those who might

eventually replace them. In the many interviews that form the
basis of this book's research, the authors heard one theme constantly: a note of profound discouragement among today's federal workers, coupled with a lack of enthusiasm for recom-
mending federal work for young people. The Volcker
Commission recognized the problem in writing its report in
1989.[16] Since then, the problem has become markedly worse if
the recurring testimony of federal employees is any guide. As
a federal employee put it, "I was proud to work for the federal government. But I would never, never encourage my child
to do so, because of the bashing [of federal employees] that
has taken place."[17] The Presidential Management Intern
Program, created in 1978 as the prime recruitment tool for lur-
ing the nation's brightest young people into federal service,
has become virtually moribund, with its slots trimmed and its
placements uncertain—so much so that many promising grad-
uates of the nation's best public management programs have
sought careers elsewhere. College recruiters have reported that
students express little interest in federal careers because, in
large part, of the burdensome hiring process and the poor
image of government work and its employees.[18] Although
some have questioned whether government really needs to
employ the best and brightest,[19] in case after case, the lack of
the right people with the right skills in the right jobs has cost
the government substantial money and has helped undermine
public confidence in government itself.

3. THE CURRENT CIVIL SERVICE SYSTEM'S STRUCTURE
AND PROCESS MAKE THE GOVERNMENT SLOW TO ADAPT IN A
QUICKLY CHANGING WORLD. The civil service system has his-
torically been based on uniform rules to promote key values.
The system has championed hiring by merit, not political
patronage; promotion by skill, not political favoritism; pay
based on position, not person; work rules clearly prescribed,
not subject to a supervisor's discretion. Uniform rules were
designed to provide equitable treatment and insulate workers
from political interference in government's routine work.

This theory, however, has little connection with reality. In fact, the presumptions of uniformity cover surprisingly varied and complex systems that govern the federal work force. In fact, the civil service system now covers only 56 percent of federal employees, a dramatic decline from the peak of 86.4 percent in 1960. Many agencies have opted out of the inflexible central system to create their own personnel policies and procedures.[20] Federal intelligence agencies, the FAA, the Postal Service, and others have obtained congressional approval to design and administer systems that respond to and support their specialized needs. The system designed to promote uniform treatment for federal employees now covers barely half of all those who work for the federal government— and none of the millions more outside the government who do its work. To complicate the problem, the agency-based experiments have often blossomed randomly, driven by the ideas of agency managers and the idiosyncratic needs of their agencies. The pressure to break free of the all-power-to-the-center civil service system has produced an equal but opposite reaction that verges on chaos and puts at risk basic values that have driven the system for more than a century.

The traditional hiring process—central personnel lists fed by centrally administered exams, or the standard SF 171 resume form used across all agencies—has been replaced by agency-based processes and internet-based job listings. Potential employees have better access to information. But the civil service system has become less *one* system than a set of often unconnected processes, with little oversight to maintain the core values that, for more than a century, undergirded it.

In fiscal year 1994, for example, the federal government hired 37,894 permanent full-time employees into the career service: 36 percent through the excepted service, for which no special examinations were available; 17 percent through OPM examinations; 12 percent through authority delegated to the agencies; 13 percent through special hiring authority; and 27 percent through other routes.[21] But even though the OPM has

delegated to agencies the authority to devise their own processes, at least on paper, success has varied widely. In many agencies, nothing really has changed: some do not have the capacity to create new hiring processes, so they have simply adopted
the OPM's old rules as their own; others still feel hamstrung by
the OPM's regulations. Delegated record keeping has accompanied delegated hiring; so it is increasingly hard to assess how
the hiring process actually works across the government. The
uniform yet complicated system has been replaced by a process
as varied as the agencies doing the hiring.

Many other special hiring authorities, too numerous to
fully catalog, further complicate this non-system. There are
nearly forty different ways to hire a temporary employee, for
example. Students with excellent undergraduate records may
be hired without examination through the Outstanding
Scholars program. Returned Peace Corps volunteers are given
special consideration. There is a direct hire authority for veterans of the war in Vietnam. All veterans are given special hiring preference, with additional points added to their examination scores and additional consideration throughout their
federal careers. These special authorities, coupled with the
agency-based hiring process, have made the system a triumph
of ad hocracy.

Despite the proliferation of such hiring arrangements,
even many government employees still presume that a standardized, centralized system governs hiring. Much of the real
responsibility for recruiting, testing, and hiring has shifted to
the agencies from OPM and its central system, but neither the
reality nor implications of this delegation are acknowledged or
well understood, especially by the OPM. The GAO, moreover,
has criticized the OPM for inadequate monitoring of the hiring
authority delegated to the agencies.[22]

Furthermore, many agencies—possibly most of them,
although no one knows for sure—do not have the resources or
the expertise to fully assume the decentralized tasks. The
OPM, in fact, has often shifted the workload to the agencies
without fundamentally changing the basic rules. Agency offi-

cials are doing jobs they are not recognized for doing. They do not have adequate resources to do them. The system frequently does not produce the right people because they are being evaluated by out-of-date criteria.

Real reform must align the needs of federal agencies with a system that provides them with the people they need to do their jobs well. The present system is not organized with this goal as its central aim. In fact the system creates roadblocks to agency managers seeking to manage their programs effectively.

4. THE CURRENT CIVIL SERVICE SYSTEM DOES NOT ADE-QUATELY MOTIVATE GOVERNMENT EMPLOYEES TO HIGH PER-FORMANCE. Government's workers often have far more flexibility than they use. Government's culture, however, discourages them from using it: there are few rewards for success and far too many risks for failure. The culture discourages government employees from attempting anything not specifically required, instead of encouraging them to experiment with anything not explicitly forbidden.[23]

There are few rewards for success beyond the intrinsic satisfaction of a job well done. The federal government's performance measurement and award system have been poorly managed. Members of Congress have frequently criticized bonuses awarded to top performers. Congress asks why employees should receive extra compensation from taxpayers simply for doing their job.

There are, moreover, large risks in failure, ranging from attack in the media to criticism from Congress, even if the failure lies in factors far beyond individuals' control. Indeed, the government's growing reliance on grantees and contractors multiplies the opportunities for problems. It reduces the ability of government employees to control the system, yet increases the need for a scapegoat. Government's own employees frequently reap the blame for problems occurring anywhere within a vast and increasingly complex system.

These conditions make the government painfully slow to learn, much too rigid in dealing with rapidly changing problems, and far too sluggish in dealing with its partners. In ways often imperceptible from the outside but painfully palpable on the inside, this culture erodes the morale of federal workers. It drives the quality of government's work down and its costs up. The existing civil service system, quite simply, contains far too few incentives for high performance and far too many incentives for workers to take the safer, lower-risk path.

5. THE CURRENT CIVIL SERVICE SYSTEM HAS BECOME A POLITICALLY USEFUL WHIPPING BOY FOR PUBLIC MANAGEMENT PROBLEMS ROOTED IN THE FEDERAL GOVERNMENT'S SYSTEM OF GOVERNANCE. Presidents Jimmy Carter and Ronald Reagan successfully ran against Washington and, by extension, the federal bureaucrats who manage government programs. (The surprising and rarely understood fact that 89 percent of all federal employees work *outside* the Washington area mattered little to this debate.) Even in the Bush and Clinton administrations, reining in bureaucratic power, cutting federal regulations and the bureaucrats who issue them, and reducing the federal work force have been trophies in the war against big government.

Of course, using either the number of government employees or the number of agencies in which they work as a meaningful target is ridiculous. Both are tools used for the critical issue: doing well what government decides to do. If voters or elected officials want a smaller government, the way to do this is to decide that government ought to do less. The government ought to have the right number of employees it needs, with the right skills in the right places, to do what has to be done. To cut first—either the size of the work force or the number of agencies—before connecting the cuts to the job to be done is to risk programs that work poorly and costs that spiral upward. Fielding a bureaucracy poorly equipped for the job to be done is like trying to dig a hole without a shovel: the job will never be done as well, quickly, or cheaply as it ought to be.

For better or worse, government employees and the agencies in which they work have nevertheless become the points by which elected officials have come to keep score of government's size. The Clinton administration has continually trumpeted the reduction in the federal work force by 272,900 employees in the first phase of its reinventing government campaign and thousands more in phase two, launched in late 1994. Congressional Republicans in 1995 attempted to trump the administration by pledging to eliminate at least four cabinet departments and to restructure other federal agencies. Even more personnel reductions would flow from such cuts.

Whatever merit there might be in cutting the federal government's size, it is hard to justify using the number of federal employees as the target. The number of federal civilian employees, in fact, has remained remarkably steady since the mid-1950s. By 1996 it stood at about 2 million workers, virtually the same as during the Kennedy administration. If there is a "big government" problem, it is a not a problem caused by or rooted in the number of government employees. The real growth of government has come through an expansion of grants, contracts, and, especially, entitlements. Cutting government employees to win quick political points not only misses the real target but also risks losing the government's leverage on where the spending increases really lie.

That, however, requires two tough commitments: focusing on highly valued, politically protected dollars, from defense and computer contracts to medicare and medicaid; and solving the tough management problems inherent in managing these programs. Elected officials have found it far easier to cut "big government" by slashing away at its most visible symbols instead of tackling its root causes. The Clinton administration, for example, pledged to eliminate needless layers of bureaucrats checking checkers. There is little evidence that any strategic work force plan actually guided the administration's downsizing, that the results matched the promise, or that the administration was tracking much more than the number of bureaucrats shown the door. In the Republican agency reduction plans, little but bold hopes supported the claims for budget savings. In fact, the most serious restructuring proposals, such as the proposed elimination of the Department of Commerce, eliminated few programs. Hence, the case for budget savings was weak indeed.

Inputs—dollars spent, agencies created or destroyed, programs passed, bureaucrats hired or "downsized"—have long been the numbers on the scoreboard of government's successes. Policymakers judge their success by how many new cops they put on the streets, how many workers job training programs reach, how many social security checks are distributed—and how many bureaucrats eliminated, how many agencies killed. It is easier to keep score this way, for the numbers are easy to measure and communicate. But they do not show the real score of the game.

In the current system, policymakers have tended to value people as costs, not assets.[24] Too many presidents and members of Congress, from both parties, have hidden their own lack of management savvy behind false symbols of size. It surely is not the fault of government employees or the civil service system in which they work that so many elected officials have used them badly. Moreover, simply fixing the system—even if the fix were simple—would scarcely remove the incentives that elected officials have to blame the government's employees when the call goes out to round up the usual suspects.

The current system's process-based approach, however, makes it far easier to resort to such tactics and far harder to talk about anything else. Any real reform must better couple the *who* of government with its *what*: who is responsible for which results. That would not eliminate the dysfunctions in the current relationship between elected officials and government's career bureaucrats. That would neither be possible (the fundamental laws of politics can scarcely be repealed) nor desirable (political constraints on the exercise of power, especially by bureaucrats, stand at the core of American democracy). But it would improve accountability to link, far more precisely, just who is responsible for which results. That would reduce (but, admittedly, certainly not eliminate) the blaming of bureaucrats for problems they did not cause. It would clarify the relationship between government officials and the government's many proxies who do its work. And it would identify more clearly what government does, especially the connections between what elected officials decide and the results their decisions produce.

Understanding Government's People Problems

The federal government thus struggles with many problems—some based in the changing nature of government work, some based in the problems with the civil service system itself, some based in the political system in which civil service rests. It would be folly to suggest that a single reform could cure all of these problems, or that fixing the civil service system itself could possibly solve problems that lie far beyond it. However, it is impossible to escape several central conclusions: the civil service system itself is plagued with deep and enduring problems; these problems are frustrating government's workers as they struggle to do their jobs; and this struggle only worsens the broader governance issues of which they are a part. Fundamental civil service reform is no magic potion for what ails governance. But governance cannot be improved without reforming the civil service.

The federal government needs a more flexible civil service system that can more easily adapt to the changing conditions it faces. What keeps government from adapting? The government's current human resources management system promotes protection over performance, and compliance over adaptation. The result is a system plagued by problems that the GAO has called "serious."[25] The search for protection has driven the system to one-size-fits-all rules that constrain managers and frustrate results. Imagine trying to write a single set of rules to accommodate a Navy shipyard, a national park, *and* the Internal Revenue Service during filing season. The rules were issued with the noblest of intentions and to prevent the possibility of abuse. Some reforms have eased the burdens of this culture, but despite reformers' efforts, the rules have unintentionally impeded the performance of government organizations, increased their operating costs, and diminished employment and career opportunities for civil servants.

For example, the federal government today must confront

—*Inflexible appointment rules* that make it difficult for federal agencies to match their needs with their workers. Government managers need to be able to hire employees far more quickly. The existing rules have sometimes proved so complex that it is easier to hire temporary workers for permanent work. Moreover, when the government does need temporary workers for seasonal or cyclical work, limits on the service of temporary employees make it hard for the government to build the flexible work force it needs. Too often, the government has to continually retrain workers for important tasks.

—*Rigid, governmentwide job qualification standards* that frustrate agencies in exercising judgment while evaluating candidates, especially college recruits. Centralized evaluation and referral procedures prevent them from making on-the-spot offers except under the narrowest of conditions.

—*A complex, arcane job classification system* that encourages and rewards narrow, technical specialization. This classification system unnaturally compartmentalizes work and impedes an agency's ability to develop and deploy multiskilled workers to meet surges and bottlenecks.

—*Formula compensation rules* that reward years of service and longevity. These formulas make permanent increases to base pay almost automatic and irrevocable. They limit performance-based financial rewards (variable and otherwise) to relatively insignificant amounts and make government *much* more expensive.

—*Reduction-in-force rules* that typically require a chain reaction of five or six separate personnel actions ("bumps and retreats") for every involuntary separation. The bumping process uproots employees and places them in jobs for which they are likely to be substantially overqualified. Last-in/first-out retention rules unduly, though unintentionally, reduce the diversity of the work force.

One could argue that these problems are necessary evils, the price of the American brand of public service. Moreover, even within the civil service rules, clever personnel managers have discovered ways to achieve the flexibility that agencies need. Many personnel officers pride themselves on finding shortcuts through the maze. However, in a rule-based system, problems are solved by writing more rules, with still more conditions and exceptions, until government managers become mired in them. Federal organizations are forced to find and follow those rules—and the side avenues to bend them when necessary—instead of doing the job. The Clinton administration has pledged to toss most of the existing governmentwide rules in the trash, but if they are simply replaced by scores of agency-level, rule-based systems, no real progress will be made. Neither the inflexibility of too many centralized rules nor the hyperflexibility of agency-based systems, ungrounded in broad principles, can truly solve the problem.

Civil service rules can always be improved by writing clearer, less complex, more flexible ones. They can be tailored to the needs of individual agencies. Greater authority can be delegated to those who must administer and apply them. In the end, though, a system based on rules still risks making conformance, not performance, the bottom line.

The Civil Service Reform Act of 1978 (CSRA) provides an object lesson. Incremental reform through better rules was its essence. The architects of the act promised—and delivered—greater delegation of authority to agencies and managers, but the delegation was still rule based, and it proved to have sharp limits. The act, for example, attempted to increase public accountability (and by implication, to decrease permanence) by making the pay of managers more contingent upon performance. This was the beginning of a variable pay compensation strategy. But by mandating the same rating-reward formula for every manager in the executive branch, the system inadvertently induced classic bureaucratic work-to-rule behavior: inflated performance appraisals, "everybody gets a little" distribution of bonuses, and ratings rotation games ("every three years it's your turn") that typically bore little relationship to performance. The result: a merit pay program almost universally reviled by managers even though it made most of them financially better off. Although managers had plenty of authority to administer that program, they had no power to adapt and tailor it. They had no stake in its success, so its failure was scarcely surprising.

The act also attempted to make it easier to fire poor performers, primarily by reducing the standards required to sustain the case. It clearly did that. However, it also imposed regulatory requirements and due process procedures (like critical performance elements and standards and improvement periods), another complex appellate system complete with its own adjudicatory agency, and, eventually, a whole new body of case law governing performance management. The act produced a system arcane and intimidating to line managers and employees alike. It requires substantial help from lawyers and paralegal personnel specialists to administer the day-to-day relations between them.

The inherent flaws of rule-based reform are perhaps most evident in the act's demonstration project provisions. Designed to encourage experimentation in human resource management, those provisions allow the Office of Personnel Management (OPM), under controlled conditions, to waive various statutory and regulatory restrictions for up to ten demonstration projects. In the years since the passage of the CSRA, however, the demonstration authority has never been fully utilized, largely because of the daunting procedural constraints. Approving a demonstration project requires public notice and hearings, inflexible project plans, and centralized oversight. One U.S. Air Force project literally took years to gain approval. Even then, federal managers faced the prospect of almost constant compliance-based reviews and second guessing.

The civil service system's overreliance on rules (even reformed ones) has had unintended consequences. Designed to ensure continuity and competence, the rules and regulations—pages and pages of them, many centrally imposed and largely standardized—have in the end forced uniform, lowest-common-denominator treatment of federal organizations and employees regardless of circumstance. It has produced a one-size-fits-all approach to human resource management that imposes *sameness* at the expense of *effectiveness.* At one time, this may have been the system's greatest strength. It has now become its greatest weakness, especially because its rule-based classification system is a poor fit for the government's changing mission.

Neither government nor its employees have fit a standardized mold. To be sure, there are routine jobs in the public service and there are some organizations in which routine tasks are the largest part of the overall function. Most Internal Revenue Service employees receive, track, and process individual tax returns. The Social Security Administration completes applications and distributes checks to older Americans month after month, year after year. Every large public organization, as does every large private organization, has routine tasks and functions that *must* be performed in a relatively stable way if the organization is to achieve some level of efficiency.

At the same time, even large organizations with predominantly routine tasks have more complex strategic functions. Managers need to think down the road to problems whose shape is only barely visible in the fog. They also need to improve even routine functions. Organizations must build an effective human resources system, a system that allows for effective administration of routine functions as well as strategic thinking to solve long-term problems.[26] An effective human resources system must also begin by recognizing that many of the people ultimately responsible for the government's work are in other places, working for other organizations, doing jobs that the government has decided that it ought not do itself, but who are ultimately responsible for how well government's programs work.

The federal government's classification system has long served as the foundation for attacking these problems.

Classification serves three important functions: it permits the placement of every federal job in an occupational series; it allows standardization of these jobs and series across government; and it links those jobs to a pay and compensation system. The system builds on the Classification Act of 1923, which initially created five compensation schedules for federal workers in the Washington area. The act emphasized narrow specialization and organizational hierarchy. By 1935 the system had attracted complaints that it was too complex and rigid. The Commission on Inquiry of Public Service Personnel observed that the system institutionalized "the most trifling differences in function or difficulty."[27]

Despite these criticisms, which were to be repeated endlessly in the years that followed, the law was extended to the entire federal service by the Ramspeck Act in 1940. Congress followed the recommendation of the first Hoover Commission to reform the act in 1949. This new law collapsed the five occupational series into two, decentralized some classification authority from the Civil Service Commission to the agencies, and created a set of "supergrades" to manage the higher civil service. It still, however, valued narrow specialization and hierarchy.

Classification has not been comprehensively reformed since that time.[28] The system defines nearly 1,000 different occupations. Wages and salaries are determined by over thirty different pay systems. The paradox is that the search for uniform treatment has created a proliferation of different, awkwardly interlocking systems.

Learning to Perform

Prudence demands that reformers recognize that no reform can resolve the lasting tension between protection and performance. But the federal government can improve the balance and improve the results that the system produces. Many government agencies have already slid quietly into these reforms. Their experiences, however, teach three lessons. First, government needs a clearer picture of its mission and the role that human resources management must play. Scattered experiments in random directions might eventually produce progress, but they are also likely to produce much wasted effort and too much frustration. Second, it is important for government to support these steps. The route will be risky, and failures could be costly. Third, the government needs to discover, far more systematically, what works best. The patience of citizens, elected officials, and even government workers themselves is wearing thin. Government needs to shorten the learning curve, to fix what is wrong by learning from what is right.

Much of American government works surprisingly well most of the time. But despite these unsung successes, the government strains under the weight of growing problems and tools totally inadequate to solve them. American government is living on borrowed time and pure luck. Unless the problems are solved, performance can only worsen, costs can only spiral upward, elected officials can only become more frustrated, and public confidence in government can only shrink. Failure is not inevitable, but to avoid it, government will have to solve the fundamental problems.

Reformers have incessantly restructured the executive branch, in a search for some formulation that would improve effectiveness. More recently, frustrated reformers have simply proposed demolishing whole departments to wipe the slate clean.[29] They have struggled to find some structure that would solve government's problems. Any restructuring inevitably simply trades one set of problems for another.[30] Even worse, many restructuring efforts simply make the problem worse because they fail to solve the basic problem: *At the core, many of government's most important problems are people problems.*

The government's people process, the civil service system, is the product of more than a century of just such tinkering. In their frustration, government reformers have too often simply condemned bureaucrats because they do not understand the system in which they work, or because they do not know what to do to fix it. With their behavior criticized and their numbers slashed, many government workers simply have left, while the morale of those who stay is often terrible.[31]

Government has already slid part way down a perilous slope that leads to lower quality. If the nation does not stop that slide soon, any future fix might come much too little, too late—and prove far more expensive. Taxpayers, already restive with rising government spending and huge deficits, could become even more angry. Halting the spiral requires that government learn the same lesson that private companies have painfully learned: performance problems are at their core people problems; building a high-performance organization requires beginning with constructing a system that values people as assets, rather than costs.[32]

The problem with the government's people process is that it has grown as a system of *hiring* but pays little attention to *performance*. Solving government's problems requires building a system that focuses first on results, not inputs. Reformers have spent too much time debating the color of the paint on the building while termites have chewed away the foundation.

The government's current people process, the civil service system, no longer helps government manage the people needed to do the people's work. It focuses on process instead of results. It promotes compliance with rules instead of strategic thinking. Government's problems unquestionably have grown larger, and the complexity of its management strategies has increased dramatically. The government's work depends on the skill of its managers, and the current system creates roadblocks, not on-ramps, for recruiting and motivating government's managers.

What America needs is a government that works. Building such a government must begin with a strong foundation: people smart enough and flexible enough to tackle and solve the rapidly changing problems that government must face. New technology offers impressive efficiencies. Restructuring can reduce costs and improve service. The real transformations, however, are social transformations.[33] *If many of the big problems are*

people problems, the real fixes have to be people-based fixes.
Government administrators are not, and cannot be, faceless
cogs in a huge bureaucratic machine. They must be the fundamental building blocks of a high-performing government.

 These administrators have critical tasks. They must manage government programs, but this increasingly means managing the networks and partnerships that produce most government services. The days are long past when any government
agency or manager could itself directly control all of the
means of delivering public programs. They must embody the
public interest. Many government reforms incorporate more
private interest and competition in the search for greater efficiency. Government is not only about administering public
programs but also about defining and pursuing the public
interest. Day in and day out, the behavior of government
employees defines what this means in practice, whether they
struggle to clean up toxic waste dumps or help supply health
care to the poor.

 Government employees simply cannot behave, or be
treated, as cogs. Nor can they act passively. For government's
programs to work, its people must play active roles in shaping—indeed, personifying—the public interest. What that really means is that government needs employees who are leaders.
Building leadership is a central element of real government
reform. Such reform, therefore, ought not to be a goal in its
own right. It is, rather, an inevitable step toward producing the
ultimate end: building a government that works. That, however, requires building a bridge between the functions that government performs and the skills government employees need
to perform them well.

CHAPTER THREE

The Challenges of Government's Future

THE RATE of social change has created culture shock for federal agencies, their staffs, and their management systems, all rooted in assumptions of stability and permanence. Most federal agencies, caught in the crossfire of great expectations and shrinking resources, have begun to confront (sometimes painfully) their turbulent environment. Extreme budget shocks, intense public hostility, disaffected workers and frustrated customers, information overload—all test the stiff, starched fabric of the federal bureaucracy.

The lessons of innovation around the government, especially from the "reinvention laboratories" licensed by the Clinton administration, are clear. Government managers too often are hamstrung by existing rules that, although they were written for good reasons, have long since outlived their usefulness. The reinvention labs have relied heavily on waivers from regulations to allow managers to manage—balanced by greater scrutiny of performance to ensure that managers produced good results in exchange for the discretion they received.[1] The case for greater discretion rests on a basic fact about the existing civil service system: no one truly understands the system and its complex rules; if no one understands its first principles, then the principles cannot guide the system's operations; and if the system cannot guide its operations, there is little alternative but a resort to an ad hocracy that pushes the government and its operations even farther away from the purposes the civil service was created to serve.

The principles of reform these cases illustrate are simple. First, it is important to know what resources the government is

33

investing in a program. Second, it is important to know how government's managers are using those resources. Third, it is important to know what results those resources produce. These principles are the bedrock of government management and the foundation for reform. The chief task of the civil service system is to serve these principles.

The principles are both fundamental in concept and deceptively difficult to implement. Often a daunting gap stretches between these straightforward principles and the befuddling problems that must be bridged. It would be naive and foolhardy to suggest that bridging the gaps will be simple. Moving from the broad principles to specific action requires imaginative steps the federal government has never taken. Many of the recommendations in this book, in fact, lie at or beyond the frontier of public management practice. If the steps are hard and uncertain, however, the basic principles define the direction in which government must move and the role its supporting processes, especially the civil service system, must play in giving citizens the government they deserve.

Civil service reform has regularly surfaced in government improvement proposals. But reform can never be a goal in its own right. It is a tool, not an end in itself. It makes sense only if it helps solve the larger problems of governance in America.

The What, How, and Who of Government

Charting the road to the future must begin by assessing the future of government, the future of bureaucracy, the future of bureaucrats and how they combine to suggest the future for governance.

The "What" of Government

American reformers so often have acted like the crew of a ship caught in a terrible storm, scurrying about the deck in a frantic search for anything that could be tossed overboard.

They know that the ship cannot remain afloat with its existing cargo, but they have too often given little thought to how best to trim the ship. What gets tossed overboard and what remains on deck become defined by what can be wrestled loose and what seems too hard to move.

Reformers have increasingly defined government—its role and functions—principally in a negative fashion. Which government functions can they eliminate? What should government *not* do? Strategic planners would naturally prefer that this decision emerge from a careful analysis of government's roles and functions. Instead, it is likely to emerge as the result of battles fought on other fronts, with government defined as what is left when the cutters slice away all that they politically can cut. What matters the most, of course, is a far-reaching political debate about what citizens want government to do and how it can best do it.

However, neither elected officials nor voters are likely to have an endless appetite for budget cutting. Citizens, at some point, are likely to want results rather than rhetoric. And if the cuts slice too deeply—if nursing home care deteriorates, weather forecasting worsens, pension funds are stolen, fraud plagues defense contracts, or any of a host of other problems—demands to make things right can only increase. There is no escape, in short, from focusing sooner or later on what government should do and how to do it better. Indeed, that is the great lesson of government reform in nations everywhere around the world. In the United States, the only real question is whether the government will confront truly fundamental reform sooner or later.

Many other nations have been at this job far longer. In New Zealand, the United Kingdom, and Australia, for example, fundamental and strategic government reform has been under way since the early 1980s. The governments have substantially cut back their public sectors, although ironically, even after the cuts, the relative size of their governments still is significantly larger than in the United States. America, in fact, ranks virtually at the bottom among industrialized countries in the size of government (measured as government spending as a share of the gross domestic product) at 36 percent, just larger than Japan. Other governments that have aggressively pursued reforms have government sectors significantly larger, even *after* their reforms. Government spending in Australia, for example is 37.6 percent of GDP; in the United Kingdom, it is 42.1 percent.[2] American reformers have invoked the experiences of other nations, especially in privatization, to drive their efforts. Other nations paradoxically have been seeking to shrink their governments to America's size.

This comparison suggests that the American debate over the size of government is misplaced. Nations everywhere have been trying to reduce the size of their public sectors, and many have hailed their efforts even though these nations have ended up with government sectors far larger than the one in the United States. Reformers around the world have focused sharply on devising new strategies for improving what government does. They have paid much less attention to size, especially as measured by the number of government employees. The future of American government requires learning this central lesson: that performance matters more than size.

The "How" of Bureaucracy

The bureaucracy on which government relies is likewise out of sync with the problems it is charged with solving. American bureaucracy builds on the foundation of legal authority: elected officials make policy and delegate authority for implementing it to career bureaucrats. The bureaucrats in turn are responsible for ensuring the programs' outcomes.

The interdependence of most government programs, however, makes it impossible for any agency to completely control the outcomes for which it is responsible. Air traffic controllers must count on the private telephone lines that link control centers; when accidents have occasionally cut those private lines, as occurred at the Newark airport in 1995, the public system has gone down. Defense Department officials build multi-agency partnerships when deploying American troops, and they supply the troops through contracts with private companies. Anything important relies on collaborative networks among agencies sharing the policy turf; effective policy implementation relies on ensuring effective cooperation among these agencies, and between the agencies and their partners in the public, private, and nonprofit sectors.

The traditional theories of bureaucracy, along with the rules derived from these theories, therefore provide little guidance about how bureaucracies should adapt to do government's jobs. Government officials have had to move from seeking control over their workers to building networks. They have had to focus on solving problems rather than on managing programs, on ensuring performance rather than simply accounting for their money. The days when any agency could control its outcomes are distant indeed. There is a stark mismatch between the existing rules of the game, based on an assumption of hierarchical control, and emerging practice, which is distinctly non-hierarchical. The future of American bureaucracy requires meshing these two elements far more neatly.

The "Who" of Government

The changing nature of government and its bureaucracy have upset long-established patterns for government workers. Reductions in force and budget cuts have replaced expectations of job stability and lifetime employment. Republicans and Democrats alike have targeted public employees in part to demonstrate their commitment to cutting the size of government and in part to reduce government's costs. Bureaucrats scarcely are an endangered species. But they are certainly not a thriving breed. Moreover, defining what they ought to do and how they ought to do it has become far more difficult in the midst of broader changes in governance.

As most government programs have come to depend on interdependent partnerships, most government bureaucrats have had to move from narrowly controlling those programs to solving the problems that hinder the partnerships. Neither the government's management systems nor its civil service systems, however, support the bridge building on which government's performance increasingly depends.

The more interdependent government programs have become, the harder it has been to find any organizational scheme that demonstrably works better than another. Government's basic processes, from rulemaking and budgeting through information management and civil service, can help or hinder solutions, but they cannot guarantee them. In the end, the growing interdependence of government programs has made most important the skill of the government employees running them. Thus the future of bureaucracy and the future of governance depend more than ever on finding, cultivating, and motivating a high-quality, high-performing public service. That is why government's central management problems are people problems.

Changing Political Architecture

Government, therefore, will have to be structured to support these changes in governance. Government organizations, like those in the private sector, are increasingly likely to be flat and loose in structure, organized around vision and values. Their leaders are likely to head temporary structures, built around a core of knowledge-based workers devoted to ensuring that the government's basic goals are achieved; much, perhaps most, of the work will be done by contracted, teleconnected contingents drawn from guilds of specialists both within and outside government. Government in the United States is, in short, likely to follow many governments around the world, in which reformers have focused on strengthening government's core while allowing the work of government to be done by whoever can best do it.

These trends will dramatically change the nation's political architecture. Traditional means of citizen access and participation in government, even such fixtures as geographically based political jurisdictions (regions, states, cities), will be overcome by events, technological and otherwise. Intergovernmental and public-private distinctions will also be blurred by the invisible connectivity of electronic government. It matters little, of course, whether the voice or face at the other end of a terminal belongs to a public employee, as long as the service is of high quality. Moreover, it is likely to matter little whether that employee works in a federal or private office building, a telecommuting center (public or private) or out of his or her home. Similarly, government is likely to move from fixed organizational boundaries to virtual relationships wired together by information systems and a common interest in managing programs. Such a virtual government will have a dramatic effect on three important elements of the federal government: participation, policy, and programs.

Participation

Everybody belongs to an interest group (or groups) of some sort, and information technology will enable people to participate much more directly in their own governance. The public will be able to voice its views electronically, providing direction and feedback to policymakers and administrators and increasing the pressure to be responsive to their wishes. If politicians seem hypersensitive to polls today, real-time polls on the World Wide Web coupled with swarms of e-mail messages will only accelerate the change. Imagine Web-based "electronic" political action groups (already emerging), unimpeded by geographic limitations, connected by the internet and their shared agendas. And on the receiving end, government itself will become more electronically wired, as it leverages technology to meet those demands—from service delivery to consensus building among contending factions. In some states new systems have already dramatically reduced waiting time for drivers' licenses and have allowed the drivers themselves to select the picture they carry on their licenses.

Policy

Political consensus building and policymaking will become even more problematic, as conflicting interests (generational, geographic, cultural, racial, socioeconomic, and so on) pit everyone against someone. Infinite demands will clash with finite resources, with government forced to play referee in the ultimate zero-sum game. Information and the creation of knowledge will replace hierarchical control as the principal means of governing this game. Government will devote a considerable share of its scarce resources to creating, storing and retrieving, integrating, and applying that knowledge in managing service delivery for the public.

Programs

Many of the functions the federal government performs today (especially those involving service delivery) will be devolved to state and local governments, delegated to private companies or nonprofit organizations through contracts, or completely privatized. As this change occurs, the federal government will evolve its own version of virtual reality—strategic partnerships and alliances with states and localities, private corporations, and other in-between entities for the delivery of goods and services.

Managing the New Policy World

Consider the government this might create. Government at all levels will become more and more "self-service." Electronic access will enable citizen-stakeholders to participate in the design of public programs, as well as their evaluation and oversight. Expert systems (readily adaptable to the "logic" of the various legal and procedural requirements that govern service delivery) will electronically empower citizens to obtain the services they want, with human involvement an exception for cases that do not fit the preprogrammed parameters. In the future most front-line government employees (or their private proxies) will deal with citizen customers by telephone, terminal, or video link, and they will have the technical means, as well as the authority and flexibility, to provide "one-stop" service to them.

Imagine then a twenty-first-century Washington, D.C., seat of a radically transformed federal government that has successfully met these extreme challenges. The city would still serve as the central node of the federal network. But the government over which it presides would be dramatically decentralized, deregulated, devolved, and distributed. It would have a federal work force a fraction of its current levels. At the same time, it would be inextricably interconnected with the private and nonprofit sectors as well as with state and local governments. Such a system, thriving amid the chaos and uncertainty of modern twenty-first-century society and fueled by a tidal wave of information, would make the 1990s seem placid by comparison. It would be a system that has finally surrendered to the paradox of complexity theory: that more control is less, that attempts by brute force to impose rule-based order and rigid structure on an inherently chaotic system make the situation worse. Government would ride the wave instead of trying to control it, abandoning the blunt instruments of bureaucratic power for more subtle tools to serve the public's interests.[3]

In this uncertainty, government would become an exercise in finding order and guiding it. It would no longer be the mechanical brain of a great positivistic machine that tries to establish social order through command and control (with its people and parts organized according to rigid roles and functions). It would instead exist as part of an open system, a system bound together not by rigid rules and formal structures but by fluid networks—of relationships and information, projects and people—that provide "connectivity" directly to the body politic.

The underlying architecture of this federal government will be more cybernetic than mechanical in metaphor. In the nucleus or core, law and policy still originate. America will still be, first and foremost, a nation of laws, and there will still be legislative and executive branches. However, their products will bear little resemblance to those cascading from Washington today. Instead of reams of rules and regulations to command and control behavior, government will exercise its power through a combination of responsibilities, resources, and results: *responsibilities*, in the form of broad mission mandates (something like the United Kingdom's citizen charters, which spell out clear goals for government programs, develop indicators for performance, and couple past results with future budgets) for states and local governments, private companies, and new performance-based public organizations engaged in the provision of public goods and services; *resources* (especially money and information) to meet those responsibilities, or at least to provide sufficient incentive that they will be met; and *results*, as defined by sets of output and outcome-based performance measures that pull instead of push government's proxies to accomplish its ends.

Politics and technology together will drive an executive branch that will be much smaller, have fewer departments and agencies, and be staffed with fewer managers and front-line employees. Hierarchical structure will continue to provide the basic skeleton of government agencies and chart the chain of accountability to elected officials. However, even government's most hierarchical organization, the military, has already begun developing strategies to improve dramatically the coordination among units pursuing related missions. The hierarchies will prove to be holding companies for critical expertise rather than the operating units that control outputs. Government and its hierarchies will need to be far more flexible to manage public programs. Government will need to reengineer itself and its programs constantly to meet the imperatives of demanding citizens and tight budgets. Organizations doing the government's business, both within and outside of government, will have to be much more flexible and elastic, rapidly expanding and contracting in response to policy changes and political demands.

This scenario is admittedly speculative and utopian. Futurists in decades past have often looked ahead to dramatic changes that, they hoped, would solve society's problems. The picture is a best-case vision, and by looking into it the nation can get some sense of the direction in which it is headed. But three points can be derived from this scenario. First, technological changes are driving the government in this direction. A more interconnected world, especially for governmental programs, seems inevitable. Second, identifying the characteristics of today's high-performing organizations, both public and private, can help government officials chart the most productive path to the future. Third and most important, for many government programs, this future has already arrived. Government today is stretched between a future whose shape is clear (even if the details are not) and a system that poorly equips it for the job to be done.

Government is unlikely to adapt by conscious choice. Rather, the nation is more likely to slide, perhaps imperceptibly, into new, pragmatic ways of coping with change. But incremental changes will not allow the government to solve its most important problems. Such an approach will prevent the nation from acquiring the capacity government needs to meet its new role, just as it has been distinctly unsuccessful in building the capacity to meet today's challenges. Small system failures will likely accumulate: cost overruns, program delays, embarrassing waste, obvious mismanagement, and citizen frustration. These microfailures will build over time into a macrocrisis. Old bureaucratic structures, rigid and rule based, work poorly in an environment beset by constant change. Their rigidity makes them increasingly brittle amid environmental stress, and their rules, devised to deal with every conceivable contingency, fail to cope with quickly developing anomalies. Elected officials and government managers alike will have to craft a new system to cope with these challenges—and the potentially huge costs of failing to manage them well. They will also have to find ways of negotiating around often imposing roadblocks that could prevent the real reform the nation needs.

Every major nation in the world, along with many American state and local governments, has confronted these changing demands for their public work force. Some demands have come from the right, such as the efforts by President Ronald Reagan, British Prime Minister Margaret Thatcher, and Canadian Prime Minister Brian Mulroney.[4] Other demands came from the left, including the reforms in New Zealand, the most dramatic in the world, which were initiated by a Labor government. (The New Zealand government, for example, identified a limited number of specific policy goals, delegated broad authority to top managers for reaching them, established tough performance measures to gauge success, and provided rewards to managers—working under contract—who met their goals.) Administrative reform has become an important policy tool for twenty-first-century governments from both fronts. And at the center of the most important reforms has been civil service reform. A participant in the New Zealand reforms discovered the "blindingly powerful and simple truth": that "the driving force for high organizational performance is human resource management."[5]

Charting a strategy for a new human resource management system, however, demands devising a strategy for coping with tough challenges that are shaping both the current operations and future policy world of government.

Downsizing

Downsizing has pervaded both the public and private sectors. There is no sign that its pace will slow in either sector or that its key demand—producing more with less—will evaporate. Tighter budgets and lower profits pressed companies to trim their costs. In 1991, 86 percent of the 4,500 largest companies in the United States reported that they had downsized in the previous five years. Governments around the world have also struggled to reduce their size and costs.[6] The United Kingdom removed more than one in five civil servants by the early 1990s.[7] In New Zealand, work force reductions totaled a staggering 50 percent.

In the United States, the Clinton administration's National Performance Review called for a reduction of 12 percent in the federal work force. Phase two of the Clinton administration's reinventing government initiative moved from asking, "How can government do what it does better?" to "What should government do?" Republican members of Congress have proposed eliminating entire agencies and cabinet departments. Downsizing in government and the private sector, at home and abroad, has become not just an intermittent but a constant force.[8]

Downsizing is not simply a matter of making across-the-board cuts and releasing those with the least government experience. That approach almost surely produces a government ill-configured and ill-equipped to do what has to be done. Careful downsizing requires planning, strategic analysis of critical skills, and the creation of incentives to acquire and retain those skills. It also requires the ability to selectively hire during downsizing, for some needs inevitably increase as government shrinks. The key is shrinking government's size while reconfiguring it to manage changing needs.

The traditionally favored method of reduction by government and most of the private sector is attrition. It is easy, relatively painless, and only involves people who were going to leave the organization anyway. A variation on attrition is buyouts: an offer of incentives to leave the organization. Buyouts and early retirement incentives were very popular in both public and private settings in the 1980s; they later provided the keystones of the Clinton administration's efforts. Governments have also frequently used hiring freezes, at least in the short term, to prevent the number of employees from swelling while deeper cuts were planned.

The law, however, limits an organization's flexibility in downsizing. Employees with the most seniority generally receive protection and those with military service get special preference. Defining "full-time equivalent" employees creates big problems in setting the target, measuring progress, and determining who is eligible for transition assistance. At the end of the cold war, as the Department of Defense struggled to reduce its civilian work force but still keep people it really needed, special congressional approval for buyouts was required to target its reductions effectively. In many other departments, however, the buyouts were not targeted, and the government lost some of its best employees.

These constraints have skewed the downsizing process in contradictory ways. Buyouts tend to be most popular with older and higher-grade employees. Mid-level employees often remain, while many lower-level employees leave. As a result, despite the Clinton administration's policy of eliminating as many mid-level positions as possible, the average grade for full-time permanent employees actually *increased* from 1992 to 1995, from a mean of 9.35 to 9.55. During this same period, when the entire full-time work force declined by about 8.5 percent, the total employment at grade 14 and above declined by only 2 percent. Some agencies, of course, saw much larger declines (NASA, 12.1 percent; Defense, 13.7 percent), but total employment at other agencies (including Justice and EPA) increased.[9]

Departmental hiring authorities also affected the results. At the Department of Agriculture, full-time employment declined nearly 9 percent, but part-time and temporary employment increased almost 8 percent. In the Department of Housing and Urban Development full-time employment was reduced by 15 percent, while the department's part-time or temporary employees increased by more than 90 percent.[10] Complex hiring rules made it difficult to determine whether and where downsizing has actually taken place. Fine-tuning it is nearly impossible.

Moreover, public management reform has sometimes become synonymous with downsizing.[11] This move has both increased the anxiety of government workers and made it harder to sustain lasting changes. Future civil servants will have to manage such downsizing effectively, as their private sector colleagues have. Government officials, meanwhile, will have to learn how to manage downsizing without undercutting the results they are trying to produce.

Devolution

Devolution of federal power to states (and, to a lesser extent, localities) has become a strong trend quite apart from the political parties in power. It presupposes a smaller core of federal civil servants. The cart has been firmly placed in front of the horse here; governmental downsizing has preceded devolution. The real lag, however, has been in planning the different nature of federal work under devolution. If the federal government devolves power to the states, what will its residual role be? It is clear that federal agencies funding state-based devolution will not be reduced to a cabinet secretary to sign checks and a clerk to mail them. But if federal responsibility is to continue, its shape is anything but clear.

Control will be lessened by a reduction in regulatory authority, but accountability will remain for the spending of federal dollars. Interaction will occur between federal managers and congressional authorizing and appropriating committees. Federal managers will also interact with the remaining central management bodies of the executive branch, and to a far greater extent than before, with state legislative and regulatory entities. Although this multiplicity of interaction has long been a staple for *some* federal bureaucrats, the number of such ties will increase dramatically. These extensive new interactions will place a premium on knowledge of "outside-the-Beltway" political, social, and economic conditions in a culturally varied nation. It will not be enough to understand the Washington, or "headquarters," players and their interests.

With a shift, however fuzzy, in the balance of power between federal and state public servants, federal civil servants will require a humbler stance and new skills of negotiation. Civil service systems must be designed to attract more sophisticated people to less powerful posts. This aim can be achieved, but only if incentives are consciously structured to make it happen. It is easy to underestimate the challenge that reorientation away from the center poses to civil servants imbued with the postwar culture of government.

Not only is there devolution of power; there is also diminution of mission or at least of prestige of mission. Large goals such as constructing the federal highway system, achieving space flight, fighting the cold war, researching disease, reducing racial discrimination, ameliorating poverty and illness on a national scale, and ensuring old-age income security created a sense of institutional unity in the civil service and, in most Americans, much of the time, some regard for the bureaucracy. Devolution may, when all is said and done, be less comprehensive than many proponents wish or intend, but it has nonetheless clearly replaced central power as a force on the march. The new ethos of the civil service will be one of flexible, but accountable, partnership with other units of government.

Contracting Out

At the same time government officials are trying to reduce the public work force and devolve power to the states, the growth of contracting out poses tough challenges. If most government agencies are structured under the assumption that a chain of command links top policymakers with lower-level policy implementers, the reality is that much of government's work increasingly is done outside its boundaries by private and nonprofit organizations. Whatever advantages in flexibility and lower cost that contracting out potentially offers, it most certainly creates very different management issues.

Although federal contracting out has increased substantially, there are no good numbers on exactly what the federal government has contracted out or how many employees are involved in contract management. Moreover, even though much government work is now performed by contractors, there are no good numbers on the number of contractors the government uses or how many employees work in this extended bureaucracy. The EPA has only about 17,000 civil servants on its payroll. Its full-time employees cost only about $830 million of the agency's $6.5 billion budget. Much of the budget goes to support privately employed workers engaged in everything from environmental cleanup to staff-level policy analysis. Such arrangements have proliferated throughout government. Some federal agencies, like the Department of Energy, are little more than shells over a far larger contractor network that performs most of the agency's work.

The budget-induced federal shutdowns of late 1995 and early 1996 placed the growth of these partnerships in high relief. The startling fact that emerged into public view, perhaps for the first time in so comprehensive a way, was not that federal employees were failing to deliver services. Everyone expected that. What *was* unexpected was that thousands of private organizations depended so heavily on federal funding that *their* delivery of services was in jeopardy. Catholic Charities, for instance, receives 62 percent of its income from government sources; private charity overall receives about 40 percent of its funds from federal sources.[12]

Suddenly, employees in thousands of businesses dependent on federal contracts also found their jobs threatened. The federal government spends $200 billion a year in buying goods and services from private contractors for everything "from software to sandwiches," as the *Washington Post* put it.[13] It would be easy to conclude that we have met the bureaucracy and, to stretch a point, it is us. These events highlight the complex question of the degree to which the public sector is already privatized—and the private sector governmentalized.

For many government organizations, moreover, the decision about what to contract was not based on a careful analysis of more efficient and productive ways to deliver services. Sometimes the political pressures to get a program out of a government agency led to reliance on contractors. Sometimes having to produce a mandated service without an adequate in-house staff led government managers to hire contractors. Sometimes government officials have used contractors to escape ceilings on the number of government employees, which did not apply to nongovernment workers. Sometimes contractors have received government work because studies have shown they could do the work better and cheaper, although contracting has spread far more quickly than such studies have been done.

Contracting poses big challenges for government managers. Government must be adept at identifying what it wants to buy, negotiating tough contracts, ensuring that competitive markets provide low prices, and monitoring the quality of what it buys.[14] Most government employees doing this work joined the government to do something else. Many of them are working "out of position," with interests, skills, and expertise that poorly match the jobs they have to do. A failure to put highly skilled and well-motivated workers into these jobs literally puts two hundred billion federal dollars at risk, yet the government does not have a clear strategy for developing the procurement skills it needs.

If the civil service were to attempt to recruit specifically for contract managers, knowing where to look would be difficult. Schools of public administration and management do not include such courses in their curricula; raiding other agencies or the private sector would not work because the skills are not there either. Only a few organizations have begun to "grow their own" contract management specialists. Hewlett-Packard has created a short training course for its employees. The Department of Defense has an in-house "university" to train its workers. In most agencies, however, contract management exists on a hope and a prayer.

The contract managers who do the work have few incentives for effective oversight. They work within a rule-bound system that poorly matches the competition-based world of contracts. These rules limit their discretion in producing success; the political system quickly blames them for any failures that occur on their watch even if the problems are rooted in the contractors' behavior or in a system inadequate to the job of overseeing such a complex system. Contract managers rarely have quality training for the jobs they must do or strong incentives to do it well. Career incentives, in fact, frequently work to induce the government's best workers to get out of contract management and into other line or staff positions as quickly as possible.

Contracting out creates new activities, new relationships, and new rewards for which there are few guidelines. At a time when it is not possible to track all of the contracting activity, the scope of the potential difficulty can only be broadly defined. The problems are potentially serious enough, however, that both the OMB and GAO have created a special watch-list of high-risk programs, many of which are contract based.

To tackle these problems, the civil service of the future could use one of three options—none of which exist at present. First, the public service could "grow its own" contract management specialists, much as the Department of Defense now does. It could hire competent people and train them on the job. Second, the public service could try to identify employment pools where it is possible to buy the necessary skills and expertise, and pursue aggressive recruiting campaigns in those pools. But such pools are rarely more than puddles. Finally, the civil service could buy its former contract managers back from the contractors who have hired them away. The public sector has always served as a training ground for private employment, so the federal government could reverse the roles. One way or another, the federal government needs to acquire the skills to manage contracts effectively if it is to shepherd scarce tax dollars.

Responding to Citizens

Citizen involvement in public organizations has increased by quantum leaps. Although citizen participation has fueled government reform since the 1960s, new tactics—total quality management, customer service standards, consumer satisfaction surveys—have radically transformed public management. The Australian government, for example, has undertaken sophisticated customer service assessment.[15] The New Zealand government has relied more on market-based systems to respond to citizens' needs, while in the United Kingdom "citizens' charters" have directly tied government management to customer service.[16] Government reformers have explicitly borrowed from the private sector to argue that, just as private managers have sought greater efficiency by getting "closer to the customer," government needed to do the same.[17]

The Clinton administration, as part of its National Performance Review, committed all federal agencies to developing customer service standards. By September 1995, 214 agencies had published standards such as the Securities and Exchange Commission's commitment to a twenty-four-hour hot line and the Peace Corps's promise to mail information about job openings within a day of a request. The Social Security Administration pledged to issue new and replacement cards within five days. The Internal Revenue Service made a commitment to mail tax refunds on paper returns in forty days, for electronic returns, within twenty-one days. Better customer service, the administration said, would help restore confidence in government.[18]

It is one thing to promulgate new standards. It is quite another, as the administration recognized, to restructure the agencies and retrain the workers to deliver on the promises. The administration's report argues, "We have to have systems designed to please customers; up to now, we've had systems that were destined to please bosses, headquarters, and management committees."[19] Top agency officials had to spend more time listening to what citizens wanted. They had to reorganize their staffs to fulfill these promises and to develop new programs to give employees the skills needed. Most of all, they had to change the culture of their agencies from a culture defined by rules to one set by service. They had to deregulate their systems and delegate authority to front-line workers so they could make decisions about how best to serve customers.

It would be easy to disparage the customer service initiative as the short-term product of a Democratic administration. In fact, the agencies that moved the fastest had already been working on improving customer service during the Republican Reagan and Bush administrations. The initiative was bipartisan and, given the commitment to customer service in private companies and foreign countries, unlikely to evaporate. Critics have also complained that government has citizens, not cus-

tomers, and that the effort was therefore wrong and danger-
ous.[20] Their concerns were twofold: the label "customer" often
worries analysts who argue correctly that government cannot
be run just like a private company; and the "customer" model
in fact glosses over the deceptively complex relationships
between government and its citizens.[21]

Despite these criticisms, it is difficult to argue with a government that tries harder to do what its citizens want done and
with citizens who as a result are happier with government's
performance. The customer service movement has barely
begun in the United States, and it raises far more questions
than it has answered so far. (Should prison inmates be treated
as "customers"? Prison analysts sometimes surprisingly suggest that the answer is yes: happier prisoners are less likely to
provoke violence against prison guards and one another.)

Nonetheless, a government focused on treating citizens
better demands different behavior from government workers
and requires a system that better develops and supports that
behavior. Government workers have frequently complained
that good customer service goes unrewarded. The budgetary
process provides no rewards for serving customers, and Congress has paid little if any attention to the initiative. If customer service is a good idea, it must be reinforced through the
incentives that matter most.

Measuring Performance

In 1993 Congress passed the Government Performance
and Results Act (GPRA). The act mandates that all federal agencies develop, by 1999, strategic plans, long-term goals, and
performance measures. Agencies, in short, will need to clearly
define their targets and an appropriate means of measuring
their progress in meeting them. Success requires not only
developing agencywide systems but also individual and team
performance systems that link each employee's efforts to the
agency's products. The current human resources system does
neither. To meet GPRA's deadlines, agencies need to build new

strategic planning processes, revamp their performance systems, and coordinate the two closely. These tasks are among the most daunting reforms that American government has ever attempted.[22]

GPRA embodies precisely the changes that have driven reforms abroad: the creation of a system that links goals with results and the integration of the government personnel system with the new results orientation. Its challenges are huge, but its potential is important. GPRA is an excellent opportunity for both agencies and their publics to carefully assess what they do and how they do it. It is also the time to align human resource management systems with other critical organizational processes. But nothing in the current system encourages this alignment.

Transforming Labor-Management Relations

Real change must also include redefined relationships between management and unions. These relationships have traditionally been confrontational in the United States; there are few examples of true partnerships in the public or private sectors. Particularly for those organizations with large numbers of unionized employees, such as the IRS and the entire Department of Defense, the opportunities for new partnerships are numerous, but the tensions have often run high. Collective bargaining is likely to concentrate on the development of performance measurement systems and how they are integrated with personnel systems.

The long and contentious history of labor-management relationships at the federal level provides little foundation for a warm partnership. The Clinton administration created a National Partnership Council as part of its "reinventing government" program. The council, however, failed to redefine fundamentally the role of the government's unions and unnecessarily angered managers' groups who were originally excluded from the bargaining. As resources become more scarce, continued failure to create collaborative arrangements will only be destructive. Downsizing can cause employees to dig in and fight change. Even the ability to mount modest reforms, such as broad-banded classification, will be constrained.

Other nations and other levels of government have adopted various approaches to this problem. In keeping with its "clean slate" reform model, New Zealand radically altered the government's relationship with unions when it created its civil service reforms. The United Kingdom followed a more collaborative path in its Next Steps reforms, while it also decentralized most of the bargaining and negotiation to the agency level. The Australians have taken a somewhat similar approach and also emphasize the development of broader policy capacity in their Department of Industrial Relations.

Abolishing public employee unions is neither likely nor desirable. But it is neither possible nor desirable that collective bargaining continue on its current path. Creating both opportunities and incentives for collaboration will be a major challenge for the federal government in the next decade. A substantial part of that task will be finding mutually satisfactory answers to basic questions. What is the purpose of union participation? How can it most effectively be used? What are its boundaries in a reformed system? Is it enough for unions just to be represented at the table? If not, what else? Perhaps the most basic question is of a slightly different variety: can traditional enemies become friends? Any serious reform, however, will have to provide answers to these tough questions.

Building Leadership

Effective management increasingly requires strong leadership from the career civil service, quite apart from the policy leadership of elected officials and political appointees. Every major study of effective change—including the ability to change an organization's culture—affirms the central significance of leaders within the organization, leaders committed to the organization's mission and effective at rallying the troops around them. The public service has never been more in need of such leadership and support. It has been reinvented, restructured, reengineered, and even shut down several times.

Although the system badly needs reform, it is nonsense to suggest that everything is falling apart. It is very important for leaders *inside* the government, as well as outside, to reinforce for employees the importance of their work. Is it important for the Forest Service to continue to protect the environment? Of course it is. Is it important for the Department of Labor's Pension and Welfare Benefits Administration to continue to protect retirement funds? Of course it is. As much as everyone hates paying taxes, is it important that the IRS does its job effectively but responsively? Of course it is. Preserving the focus on mission and effectiveness, rather than circling the wagons, is the job of leaders *inside* the public service. As public organizations undertake necessary changes, both excellent leaders and excellent managers are key; without one, the other will not succeed.

Where could such administrative leadership come from? The obvious answer is the members of the Senior Executive Service (SES). At its creation in 1978, the SES was intended to be an outstanding group of generalist executives, who would provide the crucial link between the political executives at the organization's top and the civil servants who did everything else. The SES has not fulfilled that role, nor is it likely to, at least as the system is currently configured. The structure of the civil service system undermined the SES's promise. The system recruits and rewards specialists, most often very narrow specialists. Its stovepipe career development pattern further promotes narrow specialization, not general management competence.

Most of the persons eligible for membership in the SES do not have the breadth of experience that the SES promises. Furthermore, executive skills do not magically flower overnight—or at all if career managers do not have an opportunity to develop them. If someone is consistently rewarded for being a computer expert or an attorney, rather than a leader or an executive, that person will still be a computer expert or an attorney when he or she finally reaches senior status. If that is all the service needs, no harm is done. If the service needs outstanding managerial and executive skills, however, great harm is done, not only for the present but for the future.

The gap between what public managers really do and what the civil service system prepares them for is enormous. As authority and responsibility previously held by central agencies or by overhead specialists is delegated or decentralized, the need for human resource management skills throughout the bureaucracy increases dramatically. The need to develop them before decentralization has generally not been considered, primarily because of the assumption that such skills already existed. This should not suggest that the federal government does not have good managers and executives; it does. But they are good in spite of the system, not because of it. The system frequently fails at providing emerging managers with the necessary education and training. It gives them little support when they take risks and few rewards when they succeed.

As delegation, decentralization, contracting out, and other changes have quietly proceeded, well-managed agencies recognized that the existing system constrained their ability to do a good job. They successfully lobbied for exceptions from the system and cobbled together practices that made more sense, from targeted special hiring authority to completely separate personnel systems. Such piecemeal reform creates important disparities in the civil service, with one set of agencies seizing every opportunity—and sometimes creating new ones—while another group simply falls farther and farther behind.

The system has to be redesigned to bridge the gap between the problems that all agencies face and the special steps each one needs to take to solve them. Even limited sharing of information about successful agencies and the practices their managers employ would be a constructive step. It is a clear failure of the Office of Personnel Management that it has not provided such assistance and support as agencies have struggled to become more effective and productive.

Becoming Transparent

Government decisions, under pressures both from law, the courts, and public opinion have become more transparent to the public. Laws like the Administrative Procedures Act, the Freedom of Information Act, sunshine laws, and whistle-blower legislation have been powerful tools in laying bare the inner workings of government. But the avidity of television for politically interesting information has supercharged their effects. Public feedback can be breathtakingly fast and powerful. Civil servants need to be adept in handling this environment and to have the tools at hand for speedy adaptation to rapid changes in it. The government's customer service movement only magnifies the need for quick response and a sense for managing in a fishbowl, where key decisions continually are open to public view.

Thinking Globally

Finally, economic globalization poses enormous challenges for the federal bureaucracy. Increasing partnership with business and with other units of American government is one thing. These partnerships will be stronger, more extensive, and more complex, but the tracks they run on were laid down over the course of a century. Governance in the context of a globalized economy, however, represents a change in kind, not only in degree. Global financial transactions, bouncing off satellites in seconds, rulings of regional regulatory bodies like the European Commission over the distribution of products of transnational corporations, stunning transformations in communications technology, the destruction and creation of political units (the former Soviet Union, Yugoslavia, the Quebec question)— these changes limit bureaucratic power by adding constraints and expand it by magnifying impact.

Technical specialization—engineering, communications, securities regulation, food and drug law—is no longer sufficient for functional bureaucratic decisionmaking. It must be accompanied by broad transnational economic and cultural knowledge. Dysfunctional government decisionmaking carries a higher penalty for the American economy than it used to, because of magnified global business competition. If the civil service partners to American business are not flexible and sophisticated enough to rise to this challenge, the economic damage they will incur will further erode their legitimacy among the citizenry. Virtually every activity of the federal government now has a "foreign policy" component. Much western timber cut from Forest Service land is exported. NASA's space shuttle carries foreign experiments, and agricultural price supports affect the dairy industry's international competitiveness. The potentially global impact of narrow bureaucratic actions must be incorporated into the civil service's infrastructure.

The Future of Governance

Two overwhelming themes emerge from this assessment of the current state of the civil service. First, the future, in many ways, is already here. Through incremental reforms and pragmatic adaptations, the federal government has steadily shrunk as its tasks have grown. The work force has become smaller, and the workers who are left in the government have become responsible for more projects and money. Those who call for the privatization and devolution of the federal government rarely recognize how much of it has already happened. The current system has already promoted some of the adaptation that must occur. The challenge is ensuring that such adaptation happens as a routine matter, not an exception.

Second, the federal government has not succeeded in developing the new skills and competence needed to oversee such highly leveraged activities. The cost of this failure emerges clearly in every tale of waste, fraud, and abuse headlined in newspapers and television news magazines. Reformers, however, propose even greater privatization and devolution. If the government is poorly equipped now to do what it has to do, the costs of failing to prepare for an even more challenging future could be immense.

There is a huge and growing gap between what the federal government is being asked to do and the skills its workers have in doing it. The government desperately needs to build the competence to tackle even greater future challenges. What the federal government requires is a new map for its future, drawn with coordinates based on the core values that American citizens expect from their government.

CHAPTER FOUR

A New Human Resources Model

AMERICA NEEDS a new human resources management model, one that promotes the core values of our present system while allowing managers the flexibility they need to effectively deliver services to the public. America needs a results-based government, one that focuses on performance, instead of on process or compliance. Many private companies, several state and local governments, and other nations have pioneered their own versions of such a model. A surprising number of federal agencies have already experimented with such an approach. The federal government needs now to move to a performance-based model.

Such a model ought to build on a first premise: the civil service system is a means to an end—better performance in government—rather than an end in itself. The central problem with today's civil service system is that too often an obsession with compliance has crowded out the purpose for which the civil service system was created. The foundation for real reform must be performance.

That objective leads to the second premise: the civil service system must allow for broad devolution of authority to those people producing government's goods and services, and they must be held accountable for results. Government's work ought to be done by whoever can do it best. Those who know best how to do it ought to have the flexibility to do it well. But that license ought to carry a price: accountability for results. The human resources management system of the future must build on this balance of flexibility in exchange for performance.

61

Government then needs to build on a third premise: public service must be based on arranging government services rather than delivering them. Despite the reality, the current civil service system builds on the notion that government employees do government's work. Much of government's current work, and even more of it in the future, however, is likely to occur through a vast network of partnerships among government workers, private contractors, nonprofit organizations, and state and local governments. The current system is not well suited to these networks. Real reform must improve government's capacity for managing these networks.

The first three premises lead to a fourth: the government's role as arranger means replacing the traditional but outdated organizational pyramid with a radial operating structure. Government's work depends on framing policy and ensuring that it is implemented effectively, efficiently, and responsively. Only government can achieve this aim and doing so requires a strong and competent core to ensure that government is a smart buyer of goods and services.[1] Government must build a strong capacity for managing the reality of policy implementation.

These premises pose stark challenges to government. Quite simply, government is not now equipped to manage a system in which the core arranges and the arms deliver services. Whether government moves to such a system is not open to question. It *already* has done so. Such changes are likely to accelerate, and government is already behind the curve. It badly needs to redesign itself to cope with inescapable changes. A redesigned system would build on the ten steps outlined in chapter 1:

—Redesign the federal government's central personnel agency.

—Ensure flexibility in choosing how to do the government's work.

—Rely on whoever, inside or outside government, can best produce the government's goods and services.

—Insist on accountability for results.

—Manage government's producers by new forms of contract.

—Reward good performance through performance-based compensation.

—Equip government with a powerful core.

—Build a culture of performance through career development and rotation through different work.

—Cultivate a culture of public service.

—Integrate the civil service system more tightly with the federal government's other management systems.

Let us examine each of these steps in turn.

Redesign the Federal Government's Central Personnel Agency

Office of Personnel Management Director James B. King noted, in 1993, the large gulf between the OPM's activities and its rapidly evolving responsibilities. The 1979 reforms, he wrote, were "intended to reshape [OPM's] identity from rulemaker and enforcer to developer and supporter of management systems to make the federal agencies more effective in serving the public." However, the "OPM still oversees a regulatory system based on central control, and has failed to embrace its new responsibility as a management agency."[2] Reformers intended to transform the OPM into a genuine human resources management agency.

The OPM has indeed tried to change itself, but it remains principally a regulatory agency. Some of the problems came from overt efforts, in the early Reagan years, to increase the influence of the president's appointees at the expense of civil servants. During the 1980s, its budget for personnel management was cut by almost half while the number of political appointees nearly doubled.[3] Some of the problems have come from the lack of a sense of direction. In the Clinton administration, for example, the OPM has trumpeted the elimination of the much-dreaded federal resume form, the SF-171, and has taken credit for eliminating the *Federal Personnel Manual*. Substantial authority has been delegated to agency personnel managers. Meanwhile, the OPM first helped create and then signed a contract with the U.S. Investigation Services, Inc., to conduct the government's background investigations on new government workers and officials who needed security clearances. The company was established through an employee stock ownership plan, with former OPM employees staffing and owning the new company.[4] But while the Clinton administration has worked hard to shed pieces of OPM's work, it has yet to redefine what its core mission ought to be.

The Australian civil service has been undergoing fundamental reform since the early 1980s. Its central management agency, the Public Service Commission, sees its role strategically and cyclically: strategically, in setting and pursuing the broad goals of the system; and cyclically, in setting, pursuing, and evaluating that strategy and then adjusting it if necessary. It is much to early to proclaim the Australian civil service reform a success and, in fact, the transition following the 1996 parliamentary election seriously strained the system. But the basic principles provide a useful map for the federal government (figure 4-1). The tasks, in brief, are framing the government's human resources policy, defining the skills and training workers in the skills they will need, collecting basic information on the system and its operation, monitoring and evaluating the system, discovering and promoting best practice, and using this information to adjust the strategies if necessary.

The OPM has fought through the attempts to change the balance of political appointees and career officials. In the Clinton years, it has sought to shake off the regulatory culture. But it has yet to move from what it *ought not* do to what it *should do*. The government badly needs a strategically thinking central personnel agency. Without redefining the OPM, real civil service reform cannot succeed.

As an important part of that role, the reformed OPM will need to license and oversee agency-based personnel systems. Delegated authority carries with it a responsibility to the civil service system's national goals and bedrock principles. Any agency that abuses that delegation or that fails to live up to

Figure 4-1. *Responsibilities of the Australian Public Service Commission*

—Setting an appropriate framework in the form of a policy statement, guidelines, or broad instructions, usually after consultation with operating agencies.

—Communicating and promoting that framework to people in the Australian Public Service (to develop their skills and knowledge and to foster cultural change).

—Monitoring and obtaining appropriate feedback on the implementation of the framework and how it is working in practice.

—Identifying and communicating good practice when this is appropriate and productive.

—Undertaking evaluation or promoting evaluation methodologies.

—In the light of evaluation, revising policies and recommencing the cycle where necessary.

Source: Public Service Commission, *A Framework for Human Resource Management in the Australian Public Service,* 2d ed. (Canberra, 1995), p. 11.

those standards would lose its independent authority. The OPM would judge agencies' conformance with federal standards and step in to manage the human resources system for any agency that did not measure up to its responsibilities.

Ensure Flexibility in Choosing How to Do the Government's Work

For a long time, the fundamental assumption was that government agencies ought to do government's work. Although from the nation's first days that premise had a shaky foundation in reality, it tended to frame how government officials looked on the job of government management. With World War II, however, even the hollow premise melted away. The war effort, and most of the important postwar programs, relied on the public-private networks that have since come to dominate federal management. These networks did not grow because reformers concluded that they were the best way to deliver government's services. Rather, they grew from a series of pragmatic, ad hoc decisions: to avoid having to create new government agencies; to try to produce high quality results quickly; and to respond to political pressures.

The nation has slid into this new system without a good compass or clear guidelines. Those making these decisions never intended to create a new management system, but over the last two generations, that is just what they have done. A yawning gap exists, however, between the rules of the existing system, based on the ageless assumptions of hierarchy, and the demands of the emerging system, based on flexible networks. Such networks have, through constant exceptions, become the rule. Existing regulations, however, do not promote effective management of those networks. Nor do they make it easy to sort through government's options to find the most effective way of delivering government's goods and services.

Many of these rules are designed to protect the government against political interference, from the hiring of government employees to the selection of government contractors. Government unquestionably needs greater flexibility to ensure that those who can best do government's work do the job. But tension is inherent in this principle. Granting greater flexibility can increase efficiency, but it also increases the potential for political abuse and poor performance. The traditional path to reducing the potential for abuse and inadequate service is greater regulation. Reformers need to be brutally frank that they cannot simultaneously prevent abuse and promote discretion.

Fundamental reform, however, does not require that the government choose between fundamental contradictions or, even worse, promise the impossible: high performance with no risk. Rather, the government needs a different, more productive balance between protection of fundamental values and good, efficient management. What matters most is that government and its citizens get their money's worth, within the broader fabric of American democracy. That means ensuring greater flexibility in who does government's work and how it gets done. It does not mean licensing flexibility, even efficiency, at the cost of all else. Charting and maintaining that balance is perhaps the most daunting task of civil service reform, and it is the goal on which the remaining seven steps are focused.

Rely on Whoever, Inside or Outside Government, Can Best Produce the Government's Goods and Services

One clear principle ought to define the balance between protection of fundamental values and good management: whoever can best produce government's goods and services ought to do so. Private contractors, state and local governments, nonprofit organizations, and the federal government itself can do federal work. No principle or ideology ought to shape those decisions except who can best do the work. Efficiency is one important criterion, but so too are responsiveness and equity. The federal government ought to be agnostic about the *who* of government work but fundamentally committed to the highest possible performance in the *how*.

For goods and services with clear products and competitive markets, the work ought to be put up to bid. Whoever can do the work best and cheapest, whether within government or outside it, ought to receive the contract to do it. The work would then be managed by the core to ensure that the work gets done as promised. That principle already guides public management in much of New Zealand and in several American cities. Phoenix, most notably, has for more than a decade based its production decisions on who can best perform the work. City employees bid against the private sector for the government's work. At the beginning, city employees lost most of the bids. Within a few years, the city employees beat the private sector 60 percent of the time, and the city has saved more than $35 million. Even more important, the competitive process has significantly improved productivity. As city manager Frank Fairbanks told a congressional hearing, the system has "forged new cooperation between operating level employees and management because they realized they had to share ideas and work together to create the most competitive bid."[5] Making these decisions at the federal level will be more difficult because the federal government itself directly produces relatively few services. But the basic principle—deciding what ought to be done and examining who best can do it—can drive federal policymaking just as it has in other nations and in American states and cities.

For some programs, policymakers might decide that the work ought to be done through the American intergovernmental system: devolved to state and local governments but financed by the federal government. Hundreds of years of political and administrative experience with American federalism show that the federal government can never simply write checks and abandon responsibility. No matter how broad the devolution, the federal government will retain basic responsibility for minimal national goals and basic financial integrity. That in turn also requires a competent core smart enough to balance the states' flexibility with national goals.

With work performed by contractors or state and local governments, the federal government's responsibility does not evaporate. It is, rather, transformed to ensuring that fundamental national goals are met. This task creates challenges with which the current system deals poorly: ensuring strong accountability for results.

Insist on Accountability for Results

Whether the work is performed by private contractors or federal workers, performance is the test. For private contractors, competition on price and assessment of quality would guide the process. For federal workers, performance would be no less important, but it would be based on a different process: devolution of authority to operating agencies coupled with careful measurement of results.

Devolution of civil service authority to individual agencies would depend on performance and be supervised by the new OPM. Under this model, human resources authority would be *earned*: operating flexibility as the return for results in terms of process (such as the pursuit of merit principles, conduct of testing and hiring, and management of the compensation process) and of substance (especially the connection of the process with program performance). This condition would go far to ensure that discretion is exercised responsibly. Initial "block grant" authority could be subject to a strategic plan that meets the OMB's Government Performance and Results Act's (GPRA) standards and that OPM approves. The plan would embody tangible performance objectives and hard output and outcome measures. It would be periodically reviewed to ensure that those measures are met.

These two conditions—*conformance* and *performance*—serve as the basic foundations for a truly reinvented public service, a service focusing on results rather than rules, on granting freedom as an incentive for achieving outcomes. For performance, the GPRA process ensures that policymakers will know whether managers deliver results (although there should be an initial grace period and some flexibility as agencies learn to develop measures and measurement systems that are up to this task). Conformance accountability is more difficult. It depends on internalized values, which cannot be evaluated in a rote fashion. Nevertheless, such judgments can be made by elected officials and political appointees.

What happens if either condition is not met? If freedom is the reward, then the penalty is its revocation: a forced return to the rigidity of rule-based management, supervised by the OPM. That dismal prospect, and the leverage that it would give oversight bodies, ought to deter most abuse. It would establish an accountability mechanism that in many respects is self-enforcing.

Some federal agencies have already experimented with this model, although without the results-based conditions. As noted earlier, several dozen executive branch agencies, employing 45 percent of the federal government direct-hire employees, now fall outside the broad sweep of U.S. unitary civil service statutes. These agencies include those regulating the banking industry, State Department foreign service officers, intelligence organizations, and the military academy faculty. In fact, several thousand civilian employees in the Defense Department are covered by an "excepted" civil service system described by its authorizing legislation in less than a page. These employees, however, remain subject to merit principles, as well as to the federal government's retirement and health insurance plans. The OPM still provides evaluation and oversight, measured largely against broad principles.

The rigidity of the current civil service system could not meet these agencies' needs. Although some agencies have experimented with new flexibility, their needs are no longer unique—every federal agency needs this flexibility. The pioneers have demonstrated that responsibility can be devolved, conditionally, without fear of widespread abuse. Properly combined, conformance and performance principles can form the basis for a new, results-based civil service system.

Manage Government's Producers by New Forms of Contract

Whether the work is done by public or private agents, a basic contract would govern the relationship between the government agency charged with implementing the program and those who do the work. The contract would specify the work to be done, the payment to be made, and the process by which performance would be judged. The process would be indifferent about who provides the good or service. What matters most is how well it is done. And the agent responsible for producing the good or service would be accountable according to high standards of performance.

Such contracts—although without tough performance standards and, in too many cases, without adequate oversight—currently shape the federal government's partnerships with private contractors. For work produced by government agencies, the process would be somewhat different. Like their private sector colleagues, they would be held accountable for performance. And like private organizations, public agencies doing the government's work would be managed by performance-based contracts. Workers within these federal agencies would continue to be government employees, but they would work within agency-based civil service systems that are far more flexible than the current model.

Career officials at the core would negotiate these contracts, either with outside organizations or with government agencies. In both cases, the agencies and their employees would be held to a performance-driven bottom line, negotiated in the contract. High standards of integrity would guide the employees' actions, but employees in both kinds of contracts would have substantial freedom from existing federal rules that limit their ability to compete. They would not enjoy the same due process protections as the core. They would, however, share economy-of-scale fringe benefits, the common culture, and most important, the leaders. The approach is a kind of "block grant" approach to civil service. The discretion to design and administer human resources (and other) management systems would devolve to individual federal agencies and their subordinate components. Above all, performance would be the goal, and the compensation system would reward it.

Ample precedent exists for this block grant model. It has acquired "best practice" stature among many of the most progressive private employers. Some local governments, like Phoenix, have used elements of this system to reshape their management practices. The United Kingdom, with its broad Next Steps organizations, has adopted a similar devolutionary approach to its storied civil service. New Zealand has taken the model and pressed it even further: nonpolitical "chief executive officers" run central government ministries on fixed-term employment contracts. These CEOs are accountable to their ministers for achieving contractually established results. With that responsibility, they are given almost complete authority to craft their own human resources management systems. Although both countries remain in the experimental stage, both have had encouraging early results.

In each case, the process will require government agencies to develop a corps of agency managers who are second to none in their ability and performance. So far the federal government has been especially unsuccessful in doing so. Each government agency has notable exceptions, but these managers have emerged despite, not because of, the government's human resources system. Successful management in the future will require a sophisticated strategy for building a strong career management corps in these agencies. Government agencies might well prove the most effective, efficient, equitable, and responsive means of producing government services for many tasks. But to judge which approach is best, and to ensure that the best endures, government agencies will need to focus on how to cultivate and maintain a new generation of government managers.

Reward Good Performance through Performance-Based Compensation

A government focused more clearly on results would follow four basic elements: a clear strategy to transform broad goals into specific objectives; measurement of an agency's success in meeting these objectives; broad grants of discretion to managers to design delivery systems to maximize the chances of success; and a new system for rewarding managers who perform well. Many of the nation's best-performing private companies have followed such an approach, and the federal government itself has experimented with it. The Federal Aviation

Administration, for example, has been given statutory authority to develop its own personnel and procurement systems to speed much-needed reforms of the nation's air traffic control system. The Clinton administration has proposed creating seven performance-based organizations: government agencies would receive far more personnel, procurement, and financial management flexibility in return for being held accountable for measurable performance goals.[6] In particular, workers would be eligible for quicker promotions and performance bonuses.[7]

Managers increasingly need discretion to cope with the complexities of their jobs. A hidden reality of much government today is that few if any managers can fully control the activities that determine the success of their programs, since many of those activities typically take place outside their agency's boundaries. The performance of their programs depends instead on the operation of the networks that distribute responsibility. Creating and encouraging such partnerships requires flexibility. Flexibility requires the devolution of significant authority to managers and substantial risk taking by them. To make such devolution of authority work, managers need a strong incentive system: clear objectives, careful measurement of results, financial rewards for success, and disincentives (especially the reduction of discretion) imposed for failure.

Devising performance-driven systems is hard, and the job will be even harder for the federal government because of the indirect nature of so many of its activities. Nevertheless, performance is the glue that holds the system together in nations like Australia and New Zealand, in state governments, and in the nation's best-run private companies.[8] As the General Accounting Office summarized the experiences of high-performing private companies, "Managers are given the authority to manage their people flexibly and creatively so they can focus on achieving results rather than doing things 'by the book.' They are held accountable for outcomes—for furthering the mission and vision of the organization—rather than for adhering to a set of minutely defined procedures." The key is connecting the manager and the organization's human resources system with the organization's goals, not with the rules that drive it. Meeting the organization's goals, and managing people effectively to ensure those goals are met, becomes the goal of everyone in the organization.[9] Indeed, GPRA provides a process for developing the information that such a performance-based system would require. It also provides the foundation for performance-based pay.

The Australians have demonstrated that performance measurement is a multitiered effort. It requires measurement on four levels: assessing the performance of the organization as a whole, of individual programs that the organization is assigned, of the teams of people responsible for programs, and of individual workers within the team.[10] The task is daunting; Australian government officials, along with their New Zealand colleagues who have pursued related reforms, frankly admit that they have not solved all the tough problems surrounding their performance measurement systems. But they are equally emphatic that the system enhances the ability of managers to manage and of the system to produce value.

Knowing what results the public's tax money produces, and which managers most effectively deliver value for that money, is itself an important base for installing performance measurement. Even more fundamentally, it is part of the implicit contract that real administrative reform requires: more discretion for employees in exchange for assessing the results of how employees use that discretion. Seeking higher performance, however, means that managers must take more risks. To support those risks, the compensation system must reward those who perform well. Those who do not will not keep their jobs for long; the competitive process that decides who does what work will see to that.

Equip Government with a Powerful Core

To shepherd this complex system, the federal government will need a strong but powerful core of career officials to carry the government's institutional memory, to supervise the government's vast network of partners, to ensure that the government remains a smart buyer, and to give life to the fundamental values that define public service. Elected officials and their political appointees will, of course, make policy. But to ensure that their policies are translated into results, they will need an administrative brain to supervise the process. That job rests with government's core: a cadre of top career officials carefully grown to guide the management process. This core should be permanent, but its officials would not necessarily have permanent appointments.

This core cannot, and does not need to, do everything. It does need the ability to make sure that what government wants done gets done. This administrative brain focuses on four aspects: *policy, synergy, information,* and *feedback.*

Policy

Government will need policy specialists who are functional generalists. From public health mysteries (what is the source of a mysterious virus killing rural citizens in New Mexico?) to environmental puzzles (how best should the government clean up the fifty-year legacy of nuclear weapons production?), tough problems will continue to bedevil policymakers. Government will need its own expertise to sort out competing claims about the sources of and solutions to these problems. The problems will not respect organizational boundaries, so the government's institutional memory experts will need to cross these boundaries in their careers and in their thinking. Most important, these experts will need to provide the government with intelligence to digest and interpret the information that flows in from the government's partners. No private company would dream of shaping critical policies based on data solely supplied by those trying to sell it something. Government needs to be just as smart.

Synergy

Government's work will increasingly be done through arrangements with partners. Contractors have long done everything from cleaning federal buildings to producing the military's weapons, but reformers have proposed a vast expansion of such partnerships. In their race to shrink government, government officials have increased many varieties of privatization. Meanwhile, state and local governments for decades have built public roads, provided health care, and managed public housing, all with federal money. Reformers have proposed an aggressive devolution of even more federal programs to state governments, with even more discretion on how the programs are managed. Nonprofit organizations have become central partners to many social service programs.[11] Such partnerships have become the federal government's most important management strategy, and they are likely to grow even more important.

The government's partnerships certainly cannot exist as arm's-length arrangements. They must be nurtured and, indeed, managed as *alliances*, with government and its partners sharing a common interest in—and responsibility for— their success. Government traditionally has treated these ties adversarially, partly because overly prescriptive rules sought artificial standards of impartial competition[12] and partly because government's contract monitors feared that they would personally suffer for any problems that developed. Private companies have increasingly learned that cooperative, long-term alliances with their outside partners, not tough kill-or-be-killed competition, best ensured success. This is one private sector lesson from which government could surely profit.

Information

The central nervous system of such a management strategy would be information: the transmission of goals, objectives, and strategies; the transmission of performance against those goals. The institutional memory function, moreover, depends on tapping into what happened and when. To a degree not fully appreciated, the federal government already consists of vast data warehouses. The government of the future will need even better resources to tap into those warehouses, to keep them well stocked with fresh supplies, and to tie them together so that decisionmakers and top managers can have access to the information they need to tackle crossfunctional problems.

Feedback

Finally, government will need to learn and assess what its network of partners produces. The more government builds similar partnerships—and it already is far down that road—the more it needs the capacity to measure what those partners do on the government's behalf. The federal government, however, has been steadily *dis*investing in evaluating its work. When budget cuts come, it has long been tempting to slash overhead units like planning and evaluation to protect service-production units.[13] In the process, however, the government now knows less about what it does, how well it does it, and whether the public gets its money's worth. The effort to protect public services has actually put them more at risk.

Just as smart private sector companies are working to transform their partnerships into real alliances, they are also investing in ensuring the quality of what they buy from others. Moreover, program evaluation has been an important part of many foreign government reform efforts, especially in Australia. Fully half of the Australian budget is now informed by performance measurement and program evaluation.[14] This too is a critical lesson that American government must learn.

Build a Culture of Performance through Career Development and Rotation through Different Work

Many government managers today do focus on policy, synergy, information, and feedback. They frequently do so in spite of a system that too often frustrates them. To meet its inescapable challenges, the government needs deliberately to

recruit, nurture, and reward a career staff of workers to perform these functions. That requires a radically different human
resources management system: one that is both dynamic
enough to accommodate swiftly changing needs yet rooted in
the enduring values that protect the public interest.

The government's core service would be governed by a
single set of personnel policies and procedures and subject to
standard terms and conditions of employment such as, for
example, retirement benefits. The system would provide for
considerable flexibility in appointment, deployment, compensation, and separation. The flexibility, however, would operate
within the core values and principles that ground present-day
public service. This corps would be hired through a competitive entry process. Its members would not be unionized, since
its members would be managers, but they would be provided
due process protections from arbitrary, politically motivated
action. They would also be allowed the right to organize to
present their views on training, performance standards, and
career advancement. The corps members would be held to high
standards of performance or be subject to dismissal.

Most important, in sharp contrast to today's model, the
system's members would also be treated as a single corps,
developed and managed as a strategic government resource
from entry to exit. This core federal civil service would be managed by a central human resources management agency very
different from the current Office of Personnel Management.
This new human resources agency's primary responsibility
would be to prepare and execute a strategic human resources
plan for the central civil service corps, over the entire human
resources management life cycle, from entry to exit.

The government would require careful planning and
long lead time to develop a cadre that can provide such leadership, perhaps as long as ten to fifteen years. Moreover, the
government could not leave its development to chance, as the
nation does today. The central agency would be responsible
for executing the plan, from recruiting and training to rota-
tional assignments and rank promotions, including continu-

ous training in the core values of the public service. It would help define, reinforce, and when necessary enforce the core values in the corps by developing and promoting the career development program such a system would require, managing data on the corps's composition and activity, and evaluating its performance.

Like today, those in our core civil service would be appointed to their positions and take an oath of office, but they would serve as "commissioned officers" of the federal government. Their rank would be based on their individual qualities, competencies, and achievements (rather than their position), and their rank would be portable from post to post. Roughly speaking, this corps would populate positions like today's Senior Executive Service and its various scientific, technical, and professional equivalents, as well as the top two General Schedule pay grades (GS-14s and 15s).

However, unlike today's relatively static top managers, this corps would be dynamic. It would be drawn from those who have learned the work and values of government, primarily in its radial arms. Its members would regularly change positions, among government agencies and even into positions with government's proxies. They could far more effectively work with government's contractors and state and local government partners if they had spent some time working on both sides of the alliance. All the while, however, those appointed to this corps would remain first and foremost officers of the federal government, charged with upholding the public trust and protecting its interests. They would also be subject to an "up or out" rank-in-person system, like that in the military, that would require them to continually earn the privilege of their status.

The corps would therefore have to operate as a closed system, relying on those who have come up through its ranks, and passed all of its tests, to fill its top posts. For this central corps, the values that give meaning to the notion of public service—merit, continuity, and accountability—should take precedence over all else. Flexibility must replace today's rule-based system, but to keep that flexibility on course, an "invisible hand" of organizational culture and core values must steer it. If the public and private organizations that do the work of government are to be driven by the public interest but be more free of intrusive rules, those at the center must personify those values and transmit them wherever they go.

Cultivate a Culture of Public Service

Even if much of the work of the government of the future will be done outside it, government will need a lithe but strong core to manage the partnerships responsible for government programs. Recent attacks on government make it increasingly risky to count on public spiritedness to summon the workers needed to solve government's next generation of problems. Neither can a sense of the public interest, by itself, convince much-maligned government employees to remain in government to become the leaders government requires. Government will need to make government work attractive if it is not to be handicapped by its inability to do that work well.

Government will also need far more carefully crafted structures to elicit leadership for change and renewal from within. To build this capacity, the next generation of civil servants will need three clusters of qualities: *initiative*, characterized by a willingness to exercise discretionary authority and a preference for autonomy as a work style; *strong intellectual abilities,* shaped by a broad liberal education and strong technical skills; and *a spirited desire to serve the public.* These qualities warrant special effort. They are needed to overcome a widespread public sense of federal workers' intellectual deficiencies, technological backwardness, passivity, fussy process orientation, and arrogant indifference to the public they serve. Without a special effort to overcome these perceptions, they will undermine recruitment and become self-fulfilling prophecies. The public service may never reemerge.

More than anything else, as this book has argued, America's public management problem is a people problem. Solving the people problem requires reforming the civil service system. Building a new civil service requires constructing a system for producing the leaders the system desperately needs. The system needs two kinds of leaders: careerists who will live its values; and political appointees who will give those values shape by working in partnership with the careerists.

Career Leaders

A system firmly rooted in traditional merit values, but embedded in a structure that is virtual and elastic, is the foundation for reform. But these values are not by themselves sufficient to sustain the federal government amid the chaos and uncertainty it will have to confront. It will require leadership as well.

Experience abroad and in the private sector shows that leadership is the most essential ingredient in the high-performing organization. This is especially true in an uncertain, turbulent environment, where only effective leadership can provide members with a sense of direction and values. Leadership provides the map for organizations in a quickly moving world: a shared vision, supported by clear measures of performance and aligned by strong values constantly communicated and consistently reinforced by their leaders and management systems. Indeed, leaders embody an organization's culture. They are, in effect, its DNA, communicating its central traits to its appendages.

Today's senior career leaders in the government's Senior Executive Service (SES), however, are neither developed nor managed to meet these responsibilities. The SES is composed of several thousand highly competent, extremely dedicated career executives. There are leaders among them, more by accident than by design. There is no government-wide executive development strategy, and few agency-based ones of any substance. Nor are SES members treated as a government resource. Most SES members sit at the apex of their functional specialty, having been promoted to this status simply because they were the very best technical expert in a particular law, intellectual discipline, government program, or set of administrative regulations. They are products of the same human resources management system that has produced the overspecialization that plagues the rest of the civil service. They follow narrow career paths characterized by vertical (rather than horizontal) movement. These paths are typically limited to a particular profession or occupation (budget, procurement, administration) and a particular agency. In any given year, fewer than 3 percent move laterally among government departments; most SES members never leave their home territory.[15]

These patterns do not develop leadership capacity. They contrast sharply, moreover, with the more self-conscious development strategies used in the United Kingdom, France, Germany, Canada, Australia, and New Zealand. These nations all view career leadership in the public service as a strategic issue, with a twenty-year life cycle that begins at the entry level—not when an executive position becomes vacant. They test potential leaders throughout their careers. They give them varied assignments (functional and geographic) along with increasing responsibility, sharpening and winnowing the candidate pool until those in it are ready to compete for senior posts.

The British civil service, for example, builds rank-in-person (with individual qualifications determining pay), instead of the American rank-in-position system (where the job, not individual qualifications, determines pay). British "fast streamers" are rotated geographically and functionally as they progress through the ranks. The system develops them as generalists (they call themselves "gifted amateurs," compared with U.S. technical professionals), with an emphasis on management and leadership competencies. The Australian civil service devotes a share of agency budgets to training to ensure its members are up to the jobs they must do. The American armed forces, the State Department's foreign service, and the Internal Revenue Service develop their management corps the same way. Each of these organizations actively develops its executive corps, from entry to exit, with centralized, *managed* assignments; training and development; and promotion and succession strategies. They do not rely on the passive strategy of allowing functional specialists to rise to general management positions that most government agencies employ.

Political Appointees

In the long tradition of American government, bureaucratic leadership has also come from political appointees atop government agencies. These political appointees have long served as the critical shock absorbers between elected officials and the career staff. They translate the policies created by elected officials into agency-specific details so that they can be implemented, and they oversee the execution of policy to ensure that the results match the intent. They secure the chain of accountability between the electorate and the bureaucracy's power. Political appointees, in the right numbers at the right levels, serve just as critical a leadership role as careerists.

Over the last generation, however, political appointees have steadily reached ever deeper into the bureaucracy. As Paul C. Light found, appointees grew from 451 in 1960 to 2,393 in 1992, an increase of 430 percent.[16] It is one thing to rely on political appointees to set basic agency policy. It is quite another to appoint so many political appointees that they extend deeply into an agency's middle management. These extra layers increase the distance from government's top to its bottom and can frustrate the ability of top leaders to give voice to their policies. The layers complicate the flow of information in both directions. They hinder the always difficult job of translating broad goals into specific goals and manageable objectives. They create an artificially low ceiling on the career paths for the bureaucracy's long-term officials and, therefore, impose additional frustrations on the federal government's career work force.

In the civil services of most other modern democracies, including the United Kingdom, France, Germany, Australia and New Zealand, and Japan, senior civil servants can aspire to the very highest levels of government. Political officials typically fill the top positions, but the political appointees are relatively few in number. Career civil servants occupy most of the key positions, and they are developed and managed accordingly. These countries invest a great deal in their best civil servants and expect a large return on their investment.

In contrast, federal civil servants face a glass ceiling at the top levels of their agencies. Too many of these positions are being filled by political appointees. The argument for the proliferation of political appointees is that they promote greater political responsiveness. Career officials, it is said, are less accountable: either passively slow to respond to changing political will or actively engaged in blocking policies with which they disagree. Elected officials have found it impossible to resist the temptation to push political appointees ever deeper into executive branch agencies to increase their leverage over decisions. This argument holds there is no need to invest in leadership by career executives. At best, real direction could come only from political appointees directly responsive to elected officials. At worst, stronger and more effective career leaders could frustrate the political will of elected officials.

This argument, however, is patently false. Career leadership (not just management or administration) has driven reform everywhere it has occurred: in individual federal agencies, at the state and local levels, and in other nations. This has especially been true overseas, where civil services far older than the U.S. service have demonstrated a remarkable capacity for change, and where the careerists they have produced are leading flexible, fluid, high-performing, and competitive public agencies.

The Clinton administration's reinventing government initiative pledged to tackle the problems of middle management. The administration promised to cut extra layers and to eliminate the checkers of checkers. However, the effort convinced many careerists that the administration was more interested in cutting the number of employees than in genuinely reforming middle management. It failed, moreover, to deal with the important connection between careerists and political appointees, where policy becomes reality. The failure to strengthen this connection weakened the National Performance Review and missed an important opportunity for redefining the critical role of political leadership and its link with careerists.

Establishing political leadership depends first on finding political appointees who are genuine leaders. It depends on putting the right appointees in the right places, matched with the right authority and provided with the right support. It also depends on defining just what political leadership ought to encompass. There are too many political appointees in lower- and middle-management positions, which creates roadblocks to the career paths of civil servants and often frustrates effective management.

Government needs truly effective political appointees to guide and shape policy. It needs strong and effective careerists to translate that policy into action. It needs an effective connection between them. For there to be a truly *public* service, there must be a reform that strengthens both kinds of leadership and melds it into a force to promote the public interest.

Integrate the Civil Service System More Tightly with the Federal Government's Other Management Systems

For too long, the federal government's civil service system has been treated as a stand-alone system virtually unconnected with the rest of the federal government's management system. It is little wonder that the civil service system struggles to produce good contract managers, let alone the kind of bridge builders the government will need, because it has little connection with the procurement system. It is little wonder that it is hard to build incentive-based performance systems, because the civil service operates almost completely separately from the

budgetary process and GPRA. The civil service system's iso-
lated compartmentalization is a direct product of its rule-based
legacy. What has long mattered most was compliance with the
ground rules, not what results these regulations produced. The
self-referential process produced games unconnected with the
real issues of management or governance.

Fundamental reform means that the civil service system
must be made the tool of the larger end—building a government that works—not an end in itself. The civil service system
is highly interdependent with how the government does its
work (so it must be integrated with procurement policy); it
connects closely with the government's resources (so it must
be integrated with the budgetary process); and its principal
purpose is to produce results (so it must be integrated with performance measurement). Reforms are bubbling up on all these
fronts. It is hard enough to get support for any of them, let
alone to launch, sustain, and integrate them. In the end, however, none of them can succeed if reformed independently. The
real traction in reforming governance in the United States will
come from hitching these reforms together—and ensuring that
they are all pulling as a team in the direction of better results.

CHAPTER FIVE

Guiding Principles

FRENCH NOBLEMEN traveling in colonial America marveled at the developing American character. Brissot de Warville was astonished at the easy social equality he found in public encounters between ordinary people and public officials. He was amazed that a member of Congress rode in the same stagecoach with a worker who was his constituent, and that the two sat side by side comfortably chatting together.[1] Another Frenchman was astonished at the absence of official intervention in ordinary, daily affairs.[2]

Well before the formation and development of the federal executive and the civil service system, there was a distinctly American approach to governance. This approach built most fundamentally on the nature of government officials and their relations with citizens. Citizens valued social equality, at least in principle, and they built impediments against government interference in the lives of citizens. Even though, from the beginning, citizens complained about government workers, they recognized the value of a government job, and they also recognized the need to fill these jobs with people of moral standing and intellectual ability. George Washington believed that fitness of character mattered the most in the choice of appointees. Thomas Jefferson called for leaders who reflected "a natural aristocracy" of "virtues and talents."[3]

In the two centuries since then, the American public, their presidents and members of Congress, government reformers, and scholars have argued vigorously about the proper nature of the federal bureaucracy. Should it reflect a particular require-

ment for high moral or ethical standards? Or should the
"spoils" of appointment simply belong to the victor? Should
the policy and political preferences of the elected president or
of Congress dictate the selection of workers? Or should selection be based on merit, that is, on fair and open competition for
politically neutral competence? Should the bureaucracy be significantly "representative" by geography, race, or interest
group? Or should federal workers be especially educated in
and dedicated to principles of efficient management, social
sensitivity, and "customer service"?

Since the earliest years of the republic, these questions
and others have swirled in the rough-and-tumble intersection
of American politics and culture. From time to time, height-
ened instability in the relationship between public and bureaucracy has elicited questioning, deliberation, and change. The
contentious politics and increasing incompetence produced by
the spoils system in the post–Civil War period helped secure
passage of the merit-based modern civil service in 1883. Concern about the politicization of proliferating New Deal agencies in Franklin D. Roosevelt's administration led to the passage of the Hatch Act in 1939, inaugurating a fifty-four-year
period during which federal workers were prohibited from
engaging in partisan activities. Strong public concern about
weak managerial and executive performance produced a
restructuring of promotion and compensation systems in the
Civil Service Reform Act of 1978.

There can be little doubt that the nation is in the midst of
another period of historic change for the federal bureaucracy.
Nor can there be any doubt that this change will reshape the
people who work in it. What values will undergird a reshaped
civil service? What attitudes will the public and the times
demand be elicited by its restructuring? To answer these questions, one must look at the character, scope, and magnitude of
the change occurring in the federal political environment. It is
also necessary to recognize the seriousness and intensity of the
American discussion about government's shape and purposes
that is being conducted in every civic venue. Large, not small,

changes are clearly imminent. Moreover, for the civil service, the most salient issue is not its mere organization but its very legitimacy.

How the *What* Shapes the *Who*

It seems likely that the crisis of legitimacy will be resolved only by a clearly defined consensus on the functions and accountability for performance of the federal bureaucracy. That bureaucracy will include partnerships with state and local government, business, and nonprofit organizations. Unquestionably, accountability for performance will depend on autonomy and flexibility in decisionmaking. An autonomous, flexible decisionmaker in a devolved, partnered, globalized, transparent environment must, to be effective, be highly educated, culturally sensitive, and politically sophisticated. Those requirements imply a particular set of values.

Above all, they imply that the traditional value known as "merit" has not lost significance. Indeed, insofar as merit (ideally) means seeking out the most talented citizens in a fair and open competition, it helps meet the needs of the future. Intellectual capability is a sine qua non for high performance in a complex environment. Currently the federal service does not attract and keep the smartest, most broadly educated citizens. A case can be made that, indeed, it is simply not competitive, for reasons of reputation, career and work structure, hiring methods, and pay. As the bureaucracy increasingly interacts with other sectors, its deficiencies are often revealed as incapacitating.

A primary goal of restructuring ought to be to transform processes that deter talent. For example, lifetime tenure for more challenging senior positions ought to be relinquished in favor of performance-related contracts, as has been successfully done in England and New Zealand. More rapid performance-related promotion would also support an expectation of performance. A GAO survey indicated that, of federal job applicants, "in general, the persons who accepted the federal jobs had been out of school for many years and were often unemployed."[4] To reverse this trend and reemphasize merit, it is also worth considering frontloading compensation with pay, rather than backloading it with pensions. To attract the talented and ambitious at all career stages, the job entitlement expectation and job-security orientation must be reversed.

At the time of its creation just over a century ago, the federal civil service was considered a model of modern personnel management, a grand design that separated the sometimes unseemly world of politics from the theoretically more antiseptic administration of government. Its founders intended to create a public service characterized by continuity and competence, constancy and merit, to serve as a counterweight to political pressures and patronage. If federal laws represent a covenant between the government and the governed, then the civil service was intended to be the keeper of that covenant. The covenant built on three core values—merit, continuity, and accountability—that must form the foundation for any real reform.

Merit

The U.S. civil service system was intended to forever abandon the practice of political patronage—the so-called spoils system—for all but a very few senior positions. In part, the intention was to promote continuity, but more important, it was meant to ensure that government workers had the skills and abilities necessary to administer complex federal programs. Thus the system places great value on neutral competence in service of "the government of the day" and upon selection based on merit, perhaps the most central characteristic of civil service.

However, the service's very strength and purpose have promoted weakness. A complex, rule-based approach to people and positions has subverted the principles of competence and merit. Standardized job classifications have produced volumes of rigid requirements, "by the numbers" definitions of merit and relative worth, and centralized evaluation and referral of new entrants. The challenge for reform is to preserve the principle of merit without replicating the procedural morass it bred.

Continuity

The civil service system was also designed to ensure the continued, high-quality daily operation of government, no matter the partisan political agenda. The system deliberately values stability and predictability to insulate government against the vagaries of politics. Personnel rules emphasize permanent employment to offset changing presidential administrations. Complex, legalistic protections insulate employees from arbitrary (originally defined as politically motivated) adverse action.

Such continuity is invaluable, of course, but its strength has also bred weakness: the protections against political interference have, over time, created expectation of tenure and virtually lifetime employment. These expectations derive from the very words used to initiate people into the civil service—words like "career appointment," a lofty status that, once attained, becomes an entitlement revocable only with the greatest of difficulties. The expectations also stem from a compensation system that rewards years of service more than an employee's contributions to results.

This bias toward permanence, in both security and salary, certainly serves the goal of continuity. But it no longer fits the reality of a government in which stability and predictability have disappeared. The inflexibility and inertia they engender are dysfunctional. In today's uncertain environment, flexibility is the key. This requires a work force with fewer permanent employees and lower fixed personnel costs, one that can be rapidly sized and shaped to meet competition, customer, or fiscal constraint. Indeed, the very notion of a large career federal service needs to be reexamined. The protections and entitlements that define that service were originally designed to guard against political abuses. They have, but they have ossified to the point that they undermine the performance of federal organizations and weaken the employees they were intended to protect.

Accountability

To promote merit and continuity, the civil service system has long placed great value on accountability. Americans have long distrusted government and the risks of arbitrary use of its power. The civil service system recognizes that valuing merit and continuity vests considerable power in bureaucrats. Since the mid-1880s, civil service rules have grown like kudzu to limit and constrain that power.

Rules, moreover, have been a two-edged sword to protect government employees as well as citizens. Government bureaucracy, in the United States as elsewhere, has not only been a source of power but also of employment. The reform movement sought to make clear the standards by which government workers would be hired and promoted, increase the professionalism of these workers, and insulate them from political interference. If the rules grew to limit bureaucrats' power, they also protected those who exercised that power.

Over time, however, these rules became ends in themselves, interpreted and enforced through complex accountability mechanisms that emphasized compliance over performance. Federal civil servants have traditionally been measured by how well they conform to the rules. Every incentive in the system, therefore, promotes compliance, but the compliance culture has gotten in the way of effective management.

No one wants to discard these three values, but it is painfully clear that pursuing them has gotten in the way of the results they were designed to produce. To make matters worse, fundamental changes in governance, government, and public policy are widening the gap between how government works and the challenges it must surmount. The strains are cracking the very foundation of public policy, undermining its performance, driving up its costs, and wrecking public confidence in government. It is time to launch fundamental reforms that solve these basic problems while preserving the values on which the system is based.

Barriers to Reform

The case for reform is unquestioned. Winning political consensus on any reform, however, will prove extremely difficult, for several reasons.

Dullness

In generating public and political interest, civil service reform, quite frankly, suffers from a double liability. Most observers view public management itself as not very exciting. It is often viewed as the residual after the truly interesting policy questions are decided, the routine work that can simply be left to the bureaucrats. That, of course, is scarcely the case: program after program has proved that even the clearest dreams can lead to disappointment without careful management of results. But even within public management, human resources policy induces glazed eyes. The arcane world of testing, classification, fringe benefits, general schedules, compensation, and bumping rules conspires to make the field dull and incomprehensible to anyone who has not already invested much of a lifetime in studying it.

This book has made the point about just how wrong these views are. To a far greater degree than even some of government's closest observers realize, the quality of the civil service shapes the quality of government's results. The service's manifest problems have created problems that, in turn, have worsened government's problems of public legitimacy. There is no solution to many of these problems without first rebuilding the foundation of the public service. But it is hard to make that case when the subject is viewed as an issue that is as dull as dishwater.

Incomprehensibility

The civil service system's very dullness and arcane details have created a cohort of enthusiastic fans who guard the details zealously: government bureaucrats in general and personnel managers in particular; public employee unions; and congressional committees. If the current system is unquestionably dysfunctional, its rules also make it comfortably predictable in helping workers reduce risks. Its details provide great advantage to anyone who has mastered them. They drive away outsiders, who have an extraordinarily difficult time learning enough to play the game, and they provide great power to anyone who knows enough to navigate the system or to help others to do so.

That is true of government employees who, after several years of negotiating its byways, learn how to use its intricacies to their advantage. It is true of public employee unions, whose ability to help employees (and therefore encourage them to join) increases with their knack for helping workers through the system's maze and representing them well in times of trouble. It is especially true of the handful of members of Congress and their staffs who truly understand the system and who, therefore, have enormous power in shaping the conduct of the federal government.

It is difficult to gain support for reform because those with the most immediate stakes in the system have mastered it and therefore have a great deal to lose with change. The current system has few enthusiastic supporters, but the system's dysfunctions are more comfortable than the uncertainties that real reform would bring. If nothing else, reform would upset and transform the current power relationships in which many participants have a strong and deeply vested interest. Even if reform would make their lives better, it is hard to make the case to them because it would require them to take big chances. The system is a devil, but knowing it brings comfort.

The Risks of a Performance-Based System

Performance-based reform would greatly magnify these risks. It would substitute external measures of success for internally wired levers of power and influence. It would offer substantial incentives for high-quality work, but these incentives would be balanced by substantial risks, including the very real loss of a job or a contract, if the work is not of sufficiently high quality or low cost. Public employee unions, already struggling to maintain their role and status, would face the potential loss of membership if more government work is contracted out. Members of Congress would have to put themselves on the line by defining more precisely which goals they expected public programs to achieve and by judging how well they achieved them. They would also have to restrain themselves from second-guessing the process.

Some employees could gain substantially from a transformation to a performance-based management system. Government employees who do well would gain greater flexibility in doing their jobs (itself an often underrated incentive), greater job satisfaction, and performance incentives. Contractors who compete for and win government work could find substantial rewards. Unions could find vast new sources of membership among the federal government's partners. Members of Congress could benefit from trumpeting their role in providing better value to taxpayers. In each case, however, the benefits are uncertain and diffuse, while the risks of change are real and immediate.

It is therefore difficult for potential winners, whether individuals or companies, to build enough political support for change to counter those who worry the most and would therefore fight reform the hardest. This is scarcely a government-based phenomenon; it is rather a very human phenomenon. Framing, taking, and managing risk has also proved to be the keystone of private sector reform.[5] The threat of going out of business has helped push many companies over the brink toward the reform they had to launch. In government, the stakes are different but bigger: the performance of government, the nature of governance, and the legitimacy of the public process. Those stakes simultaneously make it imperative to try and hard to start.

Discretion and Abuse

Like the private sector, government faces the unresolvable trade-off between discretion and abuse. Granting employees discretion in how to do their jobs is the only good route to efficiency, but discretion creates the chance for abuse. Preventing abuse requires rules, but writing the rules hinders discretion. There is, in the end, no clear answer to this struggle. Without a clear answer, it becomes that much harder to surmount the risks of even trying to begin reform.

The only sensible response is to seek a reasonable balance between discretion and rules. Common sense, of course, is only apparent after the fact. If employees misuse their discretion, obviously there were not enough rules. If rules create impediments to effective civil service policy, then deregulation is the answer. Private managers struggle with the same issues, but the bottom line provides a way of balancing the competing imperatives: if profits go up, then the balance must be right; if they go down, then change is needed. Government has no bottom line, at least in the narrow private-sector sense, and therefore no easy indicator of success. It also pursues many values other than profit, so even if it had a clear indicator of success there would be competing interpretations for how well it does what it does.

Government, moreover, operates in a fishbowl unlike anything surrounding private companies. Mistakes by private managers are often tossed into the trash; mistakes by government managers are featured on television news magazine shows. Private managers intentionally design a certain slack and waste into their operations to maximize efficiency. Any waste by federal agencies—or even a case that on its surface can be fashioned into a tale of abuse, no matter the redeeming underlying complexities—is fair game for a scandal-hungry media. In the face of such scrutiny, taking the chances built into civil service reform is even more risky and, therefore, even harder to generate enthusiasm for.

Scapegoating

Government bureaucracy in general, and government employees in particular, have periodically been useful scapegoats for elected officials. Policymakers have often foisted blame onto mindless bureaucrats and bloated bureaucracy instead of sharpening their own decisions or eliminating the contradictions in law. Moreover, the number of bureaucrats and the number of agencies provide clear points on which to compute the score in the game to shrink government's size. Other alternatives, no matter how much better a measure, rarely provide the same crystal-clear picture. Little wonder, then, that tallying the body counts becomes an end in itself, or that more sophisticated analysis of what truly lies at the bottom of government's performance problems fails to appear on the political radar screen.

Jumping the Barriers

The case against even attempting a reform of the federal civil service system thus is strong—so overwhelming that it has often seemed to many reformers fruitless to try. That, however, is patently not the case. Although civil service reform undoubtedly will prove extremely difficult to frame and win, the costs of not doing so, as virtually everyone who even remotely touches the system realizes, are unthinkable. No one is happy with the current system. If reform has few strong champions, leading figures from both political parties recognize that it is something that must be done (even if it is not the first thing they want to do). If the issue is not at the top of anyone's list, it is on *everyone's* list of things that must be done.

The big problem is when and how to get started. The answer to "when" is *now*. For federal government employees, the answer to "how" lies in the continual attack that they have suffered for more than fifteen years. Having been assailed as symbols of inefficiency and collected as trophies in government's downsizing, more and more of them are realizing that playing the status quo is a losing hand.

For public employee unions, which now represent about 60 percent of all federal employees,[6] reform could open new avenues for organizing workers in government's partners, especially at a time when the number of federal workers will, in any case, inevitably decline. Moreover, a performance-based management system provides a rich new field in which the unions could operate: representing workers in defining what the program objectives ought to be, which performance measures will be used, and how they will be interpreted. Indeed, the role of public employee unions could well shift dramatically from antagonism, in contesting pay and grievance issues, to a partnership, in shaping and measuring goals.

For members of Congress, civil service reform could become a handle on government reform and therefore shrinking the performance deficit. Since the reformed civil service is likely to be much smaller than the current government work force, it would provide a way of "shrinking government" without simultaneously wrecking it. Most important, reform would help move the goalposts to targets that any sensible observer would argue represent real and fundamental improvement in American government.

Getting past the blood sport of tagging government employees for the deeper problems of American governance will not be easy. The employees remain, despite whatever reforms are adopted, the most visible symbols of government. When spending cuts are made, slashing the number of government employees is the easiest: the tactic can produce real budget savings very quickly. Long-term costs could well rise as a result, for cutting those most responsible for seeing that government programs are managed well epitomizes the folly of easy short-run answers that have huge long-run costs.

At some point, however, one of two things will happen. Possibly, the budget will be balanced. Policymakers will then have to deal with angry citizens who, having been promised that budget sacrifices will solve government's core problems, discover that big performance problems remain. The pressure to solve these problems will be inescapable. It is also possible that the budget deficit will remain stubborn. Policymakers will then need to discover some new leverage on the performance problems that citizens care about. Either way, the federal government will badly need a human resources system that finds the best person for the right job, one that motivates the person to excel. Civil service reform can never, on its own, solve all of these problems. But neither can problems be solved without real and fundamental reform. The federal government and its workers need a far better human resources system and the flexibility to use it.

The nation simply cannot afford to continue seeking ambitious goals without fielding the best troops to support them. It cannot afford to handcuff these troops in how they do their jobs. The system is already hamstrung by structures, rules, and processes that get in the way of getting the job done. But neither can the government afford to grant its workers unlimited discretion. Discretion held accountable to the public interest is the standard that matters most. The key to reform is finding the right balance between discretion and control; guiding that balance with the lasting values that have long shaped the operation of American government; and finding the way to make that balance flexible enough to match the rapidly changing world in which the government must operate. America's citizens deserve a government that works. Civil service reform provides inescapable steps in producing it.

Notes

Chapter One

1. Patricia Ingraham, *The Foundation of Merit: Public Service in American Democracy* (Johns Hopkins University Press,1995), p. 34; and General Accounting Office, *Recruitment and Retention: Inadequate Federal Pay Cited as Primary Problem by Agency Officials*, GGD-90-117 (September 1990), p. 3.

2. For the Clinton administration's view, see Al Gore, *Reinventing Human Resource Management: Accompanying Report of the National Performance Review* (Washington,1993).

3. General Accounting Office, *High Risk Series: An Overview*, HR-95-1 (February 1995), pp. 11-13, 54-59.

Chapter Two

1. See National Academy of Public Administration, *Revitalizing Federal Management: Managers and Their Overburdened Systems* (Washington, 1983).

2. For an examination of these issues, see General Accounting Office, *The Public Service: Issues Affecting Its Quality, Effectiveness, Integrity, and Stewardship,* GGD-90-103 (September 1990).

3. The data come from fiscal year 1995 and do not include offsetting receipts. Grants to state and local governments for payments to individuals are counted as payments, not grants, because of their ultimate purpose. *Budget of the United States Government, Fiscal Year 1997: Historical Tables*, table 6.1; and Federal Procurement Data System, *Federal Procurement Report, Fiscal Year 1994* (Washington, 1995), p. 2.

4. See Lester M. Salamon, "Rethinking Public Management: Third-Party Government and the Changing Forms of Government Action," *Public Policy*, vol. 29 (Summer 1981), pp. 255-75; Frederick C. Mosher, "The

Changing Responsibilities and Tactics of the Federal Government," *Public Administration Review*, vol. 40 (November-December 1980), pp. 541-48; Donald F. Kettl, *Government by Proxy: (Mis?)Managing Federal Programs* (Washington: Congressional Quarterly Press, 1988); and H. Brinton Milward, "The Changing Character of the Public Sector," in James L. Perry, ed., *Handbook of Public Administration*, 2d ed. (San Francisco: Jossey-Bass, 1996), pp. 77-91.

5. See, for example, Tom Shoop, "Brave New Leadership," *Government Executive*, vol. 26 (July 1994), pp. 22-30.

6. General Accounting Office, *IRS Operations: Significant Challenges in Financial Management and Systems Modernization*, T-AIMD-96-56 (March 1996).

7. Albert B. Crenshaw, "Computer Problems Taxing IRS; Multibillion-Dollar Upgrade Off Track," *Washington Post*, March 15, 1996, p. A1.

8. General Accounting Office, Statement of Gene L. Dodaro, Assistant Comptroller General, *Tax Systems Modernization: Management and Technical Weaknesses Must Be Overcome to Achieve Success*, T-AIMD-96-75 (March 1996), pp. 1-2.

9. Donald F. Kettl, *Sharing Power: Public Governance and Private Markets* (Brookings, 1993).

10. Stephen Barr, "GAO Report Details Quiet Efforts of Gore's 'Reinvention Labs,'" *Washington Post*, March 25, 1996, p. A15; and General Accounting Office, *Management Reform: Status of Agency Reinvention Lab Efforts*, GGD-96-69 (March 1996).

11. Office of Personnel Management, *Federal Civilian Workforce Statistics: Occupations of White Collar and Blue Collar Workers,* NTIS PB94-131067 (Washington, 1994).

12. Charles Levine and Rosslyn Kleeman, "The Quiet Crisis in the American Public Service," in Patricia Ingraham and Donald Kettl, eds., *Agenda for Excellence: Public Service in America* (Chatham House, 1992), p. 214.

13. In addition, see Gregory B. Lewis, "Turnover and the Quiet Crisis in the Federal Civil Service," *Public Administration Review*, vol. 51 (March-April 1991), pp. 145-55.

14. General Accounting Office, *Recruitment and Retention: Inadequate Federal Pay Cited as Primary Problem by Agency Officials*, GGD-90-117 (September 1990).

15. General Accounting Office, *Federal Downsizing: Observations on Agencies' Implementation of the Buyout Authority*, T-GGD-95-164 (May 1995), p. 3.

16. National Commission on the Public Service (Volcker Commission), *Leadership for America: Rebuilding the Public Service* (Lexington Books, 1990).

17. Interview with author.

18. General Accounting Office, *Federal Employment: How Govern-*

ment Jobs Are Viewed on Some College Campuses, GGD-94-181 (September 1994), pp. 2-3.

19. Terry W. Cullen, "Most Federal Workers Need Only Be Competent," *Wall Street Journal,* May 21, 1986, sec. 1, p. 32.

20. Patricia W. Ingraham, *The Foundation of Merit: Public Service in American Democracy* (Johns Hopkins University Press, 1995), p. 34.

21. Data from U.S. Office of Personnel Management, Office of Communications.

22. General Accounting Office, *The Public Service: Issues Confronting the Federal Civilian Workforce,* GGD-93-53 (March 1993).

23. See, for example, National Academy of Public Administration, *Leading People in Change: Empowerment, Commitment, Accountability* (Washington, 1993).

24. For an examination of this issue, see General Accounting Office, *Civil Service Reform: Changing Times Demand New Approaches,* T-GGD-96-31 (October 1995).

25. General Accounting Office, *The Public Service,* p. 7.

26. National Academy of Public Administration, Panel on Implementing Real Change in Human Resources Management, *Alternatives for Federal Agencies: Summary Report* (Washington, 1995), p. 4.

27. Lucius Wilmerding, Jr., *Government by Merit* (McGraw-Hill, 1935), p. 57.

28. For a more comprehensive discussion of classification, see Ingraham, *The Foundation of Merit,* chap. 3; and National Academy of Public Administration, *Modernizing Federal Classification: An Opportunity for Excellence* (Washington, 1991).

29. See Donald F. Kettl and John J. DiIulio, Jr., *Cutting Government,* CPM-952 (Brookings, 1995).

30. See Craig W. Thomas, "Reorganizing Public Organizations: Alternatives, Objectives, and Evidence," *Journal of Public Administration Research and Theory,* vol. 3 (October 1993), pp. 457-86.

31. See General Accounting Office, *Transforming the Civil Service: Building the Workforce of the Future, Results of a GAO-Sponsored Symposium,* GGD-96-35 (December 1995), pp. 8-9; and Anne Laurent, "The Cutting Edge," *Government Executive,* vol. 28 (March 1996), pp. 10-19.

32. General Accounting Office, *Civil Service Reform: Changing Times Demand New Approaches,* T-GGD-96-31 (October 1995).

33. See, for example, Peter F. Drucker, *Managing in a Time of Great Change* (Truman Talley Books/Dutton, 1995), especially chap. 21.

Chapter Three

1. See General Accounting Office , *Managing for Results: Experiences Abroad Suggest Insights for Federal Management Reforms,* GGD-95-120

(May 1995); and James Thompson, "Joe vs. the Bureaucracy," *Government Executive*, vol. 27 (October 1995), pp. 50-55.

2. Organization for Economic Cooperation and Development, *Public Management Developments: Survey 1993* (Paris, 1993), p. 11.

3. Peter Senge, *The Fifth Discipline* (Doubleday, 1990), p. 64.

4. See Donald Savoie, *Thatcher, Reagan, Mulroney: In Search of a New Bureaucracy* (University of Pittsburgh Press,1994).

5. Statement of Roger Blakely, New Zealand Secretary for the Environment, before the U.S. General Accounting Office Symposium on Reinvention and Change, Washington, October 1995, p. 37.

6. National Academy of Public Administration, *Effective Downsizing: A Compendium of Lessons Learned for Government Organizations* (Washington, 1995), p. 1;General Accounting Office, *Managing for Results*, and *Deficit Reduction: Experiences of Other Nations*, AIMD-95-30 (December 1994).

7. Christopher Hood, "Deprivileging the U.K. Civil Service," in Jon Pierre, ed., *Bureaucracy in the Modern State: An Introduction to Comparative Public Administration* (Aldershot: Edmund Elgar Publishing, 1995), pp. 96-97.

8. National Academy of Public Administration, *Effective Downsizing,* p. 1.

9. OPM Central Personnel Data File.

10. Ibid.

11. Donald F. Kettl, "Building Lasting Reform: Enduring Questions, Missing Answers," in Donald F. Kettl and John J. DiIulio, eds., *Inside the Reinvention Machine: Appraising Governmental Reform* (Brookings, 1995), pp. 9-83.

12. Milt Freudenheim, "Charities Say Government Cuts Would Jeopardize Their Ability to Help the Needy," *New York Times*, February 5, 1996, p. B8.

13. Peter Behr and Martha M. Hamilton, "Federal Shutdown Starts to Take Toll on Area Businesses," *Washington Post*, November 17,1995, p. D1.

14. See Donald F. Kettl, *Sharing Power: Public Governance and Private Markets* (Brookings, 1993).

15. Task Force on Management Improvement,*The Australian Public Service Reformed: An Evaluation of a Decade of Management Reform* (Canberra: Australian Government Publishing Service, 1992), chap. 9.

16. See Jonathan Boston, ed., *The State under Contract* (Wellington, New Zealand: Bridget Williams Books,1995); and Colin Campbell and Graham K. Wilson, *The End of Whitehall: Death of a Paradigm?* (Oxford: Blackwell, 1995), pp. 136-40.

17. David Osborne and Ted Gaebler, *Reinventing Government: How the Entrepreneurial Spirit Is Transforming the Public Sector from School-*

house to Statehouse, City Hall to the Pentagon (Addison-Wesley, 1992), pp. 166-94; and Michael Barzelay with Babak J. Armajani, *Breaking through Bureaucracy: A New Vision for Managing in Government* (University of California Press, 1992).

18. National Performance Review, *Putting Customers First '95: Standards for Serving the American People* (Washington, 1995), pp. 1-4.

19. Ibid., pp. 3-4.

20. See, for example, H. George Frederickson, "Painting Bull's Eyes around Bullet Holes," *Governing*, vol. 6 (October 1992), p. 13; and Ronald C. Moe, "Let's Rediscover Government, Not Reinvent It," *Government Executive*, vol. 25 (June 1993), pp. 46-48, 60.

21. For an exploration, see Donald F. Kettl, "Building Lasting Reform," in Kettl and DiIulio, *Inside the Reinvention Machine*, pp. 53-60; and DiIulio, Garvey, and Kettl, *Improving Government Performance,* pp. 48-54.

22. National Academy of Public Administration, *Toward Useful Performance Measurement* (Washington, 1994), pp. 5-10.

Chapter Four

1. For two looks at the "smart buyer" issue, see Donald F. Kettl, *Sharing Power: Public Governance and Private Markets* (Brookings, 1993); and National Academy of Public Administration, *Setting Priorities, Getting Results: A New Direction for EPA* (Washington, 1995).

2. Quoted in Al Gore, *Office of Personnel Management: Accompanying Report of the National Performance Review* (Washington, 1993), p. 1.

3. Ibid., p. 2.

4. Stephen Barr, "OPM, in a First, Acts to Convert an Operation into Private Firm," *Washington Post*, April 14, 1996, p. A4.

5. Testimony of Frank Fairbanks in Hearings before the House Committee on Government Reform and Oversight and the Senate Committee on Governmental Affairs. 104 Cong. 2 sess. (Government Printing Office, 1996), p. 6. See also Jim Flanagan and Bob Wingenroth, "Phoenix Manages for Performance Results," *PA Times*, March 1, 1996, pp. 1, 3.

6. Office of Management and Budget, *Budget Supplement: Fiscal Year 1997* (Washington, 1996), pp. 133-34.

7. Mike Causey, "Upside, Downside," *Washington Post*, April 3, 1996, p. B2.

8. Management Advisory Board, *Ongoing Reform in the Australian Public Service* (Canberra: Australian Government Publishing Service, October 1994).

9. General Accounting Office, *Civil Service Reform: Changing Times Demand New Approaches*, GAO/T-GGD-96-31 (October 1995), pp. 3-4.

10. Australian Public Service Commission, *Managing People's Performance: Advice for Managers* (Canberra, 1994).

11. Steven Rathgeb Smith and Michael Lipsky, *Nonprofits for Hire: The Welfare State in the Age of Contracting* (Harvard University Press, 1993).

12. Steven Kelman, *Procurement and Public Management: The Fear of Discretion and the Quality of Government Performance* (Washington: AEI Press, 1990).

13. General Accounting Office, *Federal Evaluation: Fewer Units, Reduced Resources, Different Studies from 1980*, PEMD-87-9 (January 1987); and Office of Management and Budget, *Interagency Task Force Report on the Federal Contract Audit Process* (Washington, December 1992).

14. Kim C. Beazley, "Briefing for Public Sector Senior Managers," Brisbane, July 14, 1994, p. 4.

15. Paul C. Light, *Thickening Government: Federal Hierarchy and the Diffusion of Accountability* (Brookings, 1995), p. 67.

16. Light, *Thickening Government*, p. 7.

Chapter Five

1. Catherine Drinker Bowen, *Miracle at Philadelphia: The Story of the Constitutional Convention, May to September 1787* (Little, Brown, and Co., 1966), pp. 153–54; and Patricia W. Ingraham, *The Foundation of Merit: Public Service in American Democracy* (Johns Hopkins University Press, 1995), pp. 17, 19.

2. Ibid., p. 155.

3. Ingraham, *The Foundation of Merit*, pp. 17,19.

4. General Accounting Office, *The Public Service: Issues Confronting the Federal Civilian Workforce*, GGD-94-157 (August 1994), p. 7.

5. See, for example, James Champy, *Reengineering Management: The Mandate for New Leadership* (HarperBusiness, 1995).

6. Carolyn Ban, "Unions, Management, and the NPR," in Donald F. Kettl and John J. DiIulio, eds., *Inside the Reinvention Machine*: *Appraising Governmental Reform* (Brookings, 1995), p. 132.

Index

Accountability: civil service system and, 92; contracting, 70-72; devolution of power to states, 6, 47; methods for, 25; political appointees and, 83; principles of, 4, 22-23, 61, 68-69
ACWA. *See* Administrative Careers with America exam
Administrative Careers with America exam (ACWA), 17
Administrative Procedures Act, 58
Agencies: customer service standards, 52; devolution of civil service authority to, 69-70, 71; elimination of, 21-22, 29, 45; flexibility of, 70; interdependence of, 36-37, 38; managers, 72; personnel policies, 17-19, 64-65; problem solving, 37-38; reforms of, 10-11, 14, 28-29, 57, 59; routine tasks, 27. *See also* Civil service; Government, federal; individual agencies
Appointees, 63, 64, 83-85
Australia: civil service, 64, 65*f*, 83-84; development strategies, 82; government reform, 35; government spending, 36; labor issues, 55; performance measurement/program evaluation, 74, 77; response to citizens, 51

Budget issues: cutbacks and cutting, 33, 35, 77, 98-99; hiring and firing, 17-18, 21-22
Bureaucracy. *See* Agencies; Civil service; Government, federal

Bush (George) administration, 20
Business issues: alliances, 76; downsizing, 44; leadership, 81; management systems, 71; performance, 73-74

Canada, 82
Carter, Jimmy, 20
Catholic Charities, 49
Civil Service: classification system, 15, 24, 27-28, 46, 55, 90-91; compensation, 24, 25-26, 71, 72-74, 90, 91; dysfunction and problems of, 3, 6-7, 11-25, 38; effectiveness, 1, 3; glass ceiling, 84; management of, 5, 78-79; morale of, 16, 20, 30, 56, 80, 97-98; motivation by, 19-20; placement/entrance process, 1, 17-18; political values and, 11; purpose and role, 1, 9-10, 17, 33-34, 37-38, 86, 89, 90; quality and behavior of workers, 14-16, 31, 38, 50, 59-60, 77-78, 80-83, 89; recruitment and separation, 1, 24-25, 26, 37, 45-46, 50, 55, 89-90; structure and process, 16-19, 29, 85-86, 89, 91; training, 52. *See also* Agencies; Government, federal; Merit system; Office of Personnel Management; Reforms
Civil Service Reform Act of *1978* (CSRA), 25, 88
Classification Act of *1923,* 28
Clinton (Bill) administration: delegation of responsibilities, 10-11; federal employee buyout, 15, 46; gov-